ADULT STUDENTS "AT-RISK"

Critical Studies in Education and Culture Series

Beyond Liberation and Excellence: Reconstructing the Public Discourse on Education
David E. Purpel and Svi Shapiro

Schooling in a "Total Institution": Critical Perspectives on Prison Education
Howard S. Davidson, editor

Simulation, Spectacle, and the Ironies of Education Reform
Guy Senese with Ralph Page

Repositioning Feminism and Education: Perspectives on Educating for Social Change
Janice Jipson, Petra Munro, Susan Victor, Karen Froude Jones, and Gretchen Freed-Rowland

Culture, Politics, and Irish School Dropouts: Constructing Political Identities
G. Honor Fagan

Anti-Racism, Feminism, and Critical Approaches to Education
Roxana Ng, Pat Staton, and Joyce Scane

Beyond Comfort Zones in Multiculturalism: Confronting the Politics of Privilege
Sandra Jackson and José Solís, editors

Culture and Difference: Critical Perspectives on the Bicultural Experience in the United States
Antonia Darder

Poststructuralism, Politics and Education
Michael Peters

Weaving a Tapestry of Resistance: The Places, Power, and Poetry of a Sustainable Society
Sharon Sutton

Counselor Education for the Twenty-First Century
Susan J. Brotherton

Positioning Subjects: Psychoanalysis and Critical Educational Studies
Stephen Appel

ADULT STUDENTS "AT-RISK"

Culture Bias in Higher Education

Timothy William Quinnan

Foreword by William G. Tierney

Critical Studies in Education and Culture Series
Edited by Henry A. Giroux and Paulo Freire

BERGIN & GARVEY
Westport, Connecticut • London

Library of Congress Cataloging-in-Publication Data

Quinnan, Timothy William, 1961–
    Adult students "at-risk" : culture bias in higher education /
Timothy William Quinnan ; foreword by William G. Tierney.
        p.   cm.—(Critical studies in education and culture series,
    ISSN 1064–8615)
    Includes bibliographical references and index.
    ISBN 0–89789–521–5 (alk. paper).—ISBN 0–89789–522–3 (pbk. :
alk. paper)
    1. Adult education—United States. 2. Education, Higher—United
States. 3. Age discrimination—United States. 4. Critical theory.
I. Title. II. Series.
LC5251.Q55 1997
374—dc21   97–216

British Library Cataloguing in Publication Data is available.

Library of Congress Catalog Card Number: 97–216
ISBN: 0–89789–521–5
        0–89789–522–3 (pbk.)
ISSN: 1064–8615

First published in 1997

Bergin & Garvey, 88 Post Road West, Westport, CT 06881
An imprint of Greenwood Publishing Group, Inc.

Printed in the United States of America

The paper used in this book complies with the
Permanent Paper Standard issued by the National
Information Standards Organization (Z39.48–1984).

10 9 8 7 6 5 4 3 2 1

Copyright Acknowledgment

The author and publisher gratefully acknowledge permission for use of the following
material:

Excerpts from *Closing the Doors: Stories of Struggle at U.C.* by M. Stephens in a 1993
report prepared by the College of Arts and Sciences, University of Cincinnati.

Contents

Series Foreword

Educational reform has fallen upon hard times. The traditional assumption that schooling is fundamentally tied to the imperatives of citizenship designed to educate students to exercise civic leadership and public service has been eroded. The schools are now the key institution for producing professional, technically trained, credentialized workers for whom the demands of citizenship are subordinated to the vicissitudes of the marketplace and the commercial public sphere. Given the current corporate and right wing assault on public and higher education coupled with the emergence of a moral and political climate that has shifted to a new Social Darwinism, the issues which framed the democratic meaning, purpose, and use to which education might aspire have been displaced by more vocational and narrowly ideological considerations.

The war waged against the possibilities of an education wedded to the precepts of a real democracy is not merely ideological. Against the backdrop of reduced funding for public schooling, the call for privatization, vouchers, cultural uniformity, and choice, there are the often ignored larger social realities of material power and oppression. On the national level, there has been a vast resurgence of racism. This is evident in the passing of anti-immigration laws such as Proposition 187 in California, the dismantling of the welfare state, the demonization of black youth that is taking place in the popular media, and the remarkable attention provided by the media to forms of race talk that argue for the intellectual inferiority of blacks or dismiss calls for racial justice as simply a holdover from the "morally bankrupt" legacy of the 1960s.

Poverty is on the rise among children in the United States, with 20 percent of all children under the age of eighteen living below the poverty line. Unemployment is growing at an alarming rate for poor youth of color, especially in the urban centers. While black youth are policed and disciplined in and out of the nation's schools, conservative and liberal educators define education through the ethically limp discourses of privatization, national standards, and global competitiveness.

Many writers in the critical education tradition have attempted to challenge the right wing fundamentalism behind educational and social reform in both the United States and abroad while simultaneously providing ethical signposts for a public discourse about education and democracy that is both prophetic and transformative. Eschewing traditional categories, a diverse number of critical theorists and educators have successfully exposed the political and ethical implications of the cynicism and despair that has become endemic to the discourse of schooling and civic life. In its place, such educators strive to provide a language of hope that inextricably links the struggle over schooling to understanding and transforming our present social and cultural dangers.

At the risk of overgeneralizing, both cultural studies theorists and critical educators have emphasized the importance of understanding theory as the grounded basis for "intervening into contexts and power . . . in order to enable people to act more strategically in ways that may change their context for the better."[1] Moreover, theorists in both fields have argued for the primacy of the political by calling for and struggling to produce critical public spaces, regardless of how fleeting they may be, in which "popular cultural resistance is explored as a form of political resistance."[2] Such writers have analyzed the challenges that teachers will have to face in redefining a new mission for education, one that is linked to honoring the experiences, concerns, and diverse histories and languages that give expression to the multiple narratives that engage and challenge the legacy of democracy.

Equally significant is the insight of recent critical educational work that connects the politics of difference with concrete strategies for addressing the crucial relationships between schooling and the economy, and citizenship and the politics or meaning in communities of multicultural, multiracial, and multilingual schools.

Critical Studies in Education and Culture attempts to address and demonstrate how scholars working in the fields of cultural studies and critical pedagogy might join together in a radical project and practice informed by theoretically rigorous discourses that affirm the critical but refuse the cynical, and establish hope as central to a critical pedagogical and political practice but eschew a romantic utopianism. Central to such a project is the issue of how pedagogy might provide cultural studies theorists and educators with an opportunity to engage pedagogical practices that are not only transdisciplinary, transgressive, and oppositional, but also connected to a wider project designed to further racial, economic, and political democracy.[3] By taking seriously the relations between culture and power, we further the possibilities of resistance, struggle, and change.

Critical Studies in Education and Culture is committed to publishing work that opens a narrative space that affirms the contextual and the specific while simultaneously recognizing the ways in which such spaces are shot through with issues of power. The series attempts to continue an important legacy of theoretical work in cultural studies in which related debates on pedagogy are understood and addressed within the larger context of social responsibility, civic courage, and the reconstruction of democratic public life. We must keep in mind Raymond Williams's insight that the "deepest impulse (informing cultural politics) is the desire to make learning part of the process of social change itself."[4] Education as a cultural pedagogical practice takes place across multiple sites, which include not only schools and universities but also the mass media, popular culture, and other public spheres, and signals how within diverse contexts, education makes us both subjects of and subject to relations of power.

This series challenges the current return to the primacy of market values and simultaneous retreat from politics so evident in the recent work of educational theorists, legislators, and policy analysts. Professional relegitimation in a troubled time seems to be the order of the day as an increasing number of academics both refuse to recognize public and higher education as critical public spheres and offer little or no resistance to the ongoing vocationalization of schooling, the continuing evisceration of the intellectual labor force, and the current assaults on the working poor, the elderly, and women and children.[5]

Emphasizing the centrality of politics, culture, and power, *Critical Studies in Education and Culture* will deal with pedagogical issues that contribute in imaginative and transformative ways to our understanding of how critical knowledge, democratic values, and social practices can provide a basis for teachers, students, and other cultural workers to redefine their role as engaged and public intellectuals. Each volume will attempt to rethink the relationship between language and experience, pedagogy and human agency, and ethics and social responsibility as part of a larger project for engaging and deepening the prospects of democratic schooling in a multiracial and multicultural society. *Critical Studies in Education and Culture* takes on the responsibility of witnessing and addressing the most pressing problems of public schooling and civic life, and engages culture as a crucial site and strategic force for productive social change.

Henry A. Giroux

NOTES

1. Lawrence Grossberg, "Toward a Genealogy of the State of Cultural Studies," in Cary Nelson and Dilip Parameshwar Gaonkar, eds. *Disciplinarity and Dissent in Cultural Studies* (New York: Routledge, 1996), p. 143.

2. David Bailey and Stuart Hall, "The Vertigo of Displacement," *Ten* 8(2):3 (1992), p. 19.

3. My notion of transdisciplinary comes from Mas'ud Zavarzadeh and Donald Morton, "Theory, Pedagogy, Politics: The Crisis of the 'Subject' in the Humanities," in *Theory Pedagogy Politics: Texts for Change*, Mas'ud Zavarzadeh and Donald Morton, eds. (Urbana: University of Illinois Press, 1992) p. 10. At issue here is neither ignoring the boundaries of discipline-based knowledge nor simply fusing different disciplines, but creating theoretical paradigms, questions, and knowledge that cannot be taken up within the policed boundaries of the existing disciplines.

4. Raymond Williams, "Adult Education and Social Change," in *What I Came to Say* (London: Hutchinson-Radus, 1989), p. 158.

5. The term "professional legitimation" comes from a personal correspondence with Professor Jeff Williams of East Carolina University.

Foreword

Colleges and universities have always had a difficult time dealing with people on the margins—women, people of color, the physically challenged, and adult students. Frequently, such individuals have been excluded from academe's portals and the result has often been the creation of alternative institutions such as women's colleges or tribally controlled community colleges for Native Americans. At other times, the force of law has made postsecondary institutions adapt to changing clienteles. Affirmative action opened up search and admission processes in ways that were unthinkable only a generation ago. Campuses have struggled to become more accessible to those in wheelchairs or those who have other physical challenges due to the disabilities Act.

Perhaps the most widespread policy change in academe came with the initiation of the GI Bill where returning adults had the possibility of attaining a college degree. The academic ranks swelled with returning soldiers in search of a degree and a job. Older returning students that populated academe's campuses after World War II for a time also changed the nature of the campus. Such students were more focused and less immature. The interaction and benefits, of course, were mutual. Adult students had the privilege of going to college and studying for a bachelor's degree. The campuses had the benefit of their wisdom and experience.

In the late twentieth century we often forget that an academic "community" of necessity is a collection of diverse individuals and groups. To the extent that we divide groups between "us" and "them" being the mainstream, and "them" anyone who is not—we fall short of what we mean by community. Real communities, like families, can not exist with such facile divides. One thrust of my work over the last decade has been to point out how our academic communities cannot succeed when we seek to separate, ignore, or defeat those with whom we disagree with or who are different. Instead, to enhance the notion of community, of agape, we must be able to think of "them" as part of "us."

Timothy Quinnan's work offers clues about how to increase community for all of us as we think about the experiences of adult students on college campuses. He challenges us to consider if academe meets the social and cultural expectations of adult students and then points out how we often fall short. By using critical theory and a postmodern lens he investigates the experiences of adults to show how "one size does not fit all." If academe is to succeed, then, out of necessity we must discover ways to develop curricular, pedagogic, and cultural activities that appeal to diverse groups rather than the chosen few.

Often, when I have employed a critical postmodern perspective, my critics have suggested that the work is imbued with a sense of pessimism, when in fact, I have struggled to portray the opposite attitude. It is as if some colleagues would prefer that we not point out the flaws in our system so that we may then assume that the organization is healthy and trouble-free. However, we ought not gloss over the challenges that confront individuals such as those who are returning adult students. Critique is important, essential, if we are to improve.

At the same time, we should not paint such a dark portrait that we assume nothing has changed, and any real improvement is impossible. Critical theory is not a stance of pessimism, but of hope. When we look back on the twentieth century we will see academic organizations that opened their doors in ways unheard of at the start of the century. Who would have thought that a black man would be president of a major university, or that gay and lesbian students could fly a banner from Old Main during Gay Pride Week? Adult students, though still not part of "us," at least have the potential to be on campus today; at the turn of the century there was no likelihood. We move forward, then, with a realistic fear that we might regress, that we might not improve, but also with an equally realistic hope that we will continue to change the academy and make it more equitable, more welcoming, and more capable of producing academic excellence for everyone, not merely those who reside in the "mainstream."

In order to improve we need to consider our language, our policies, and our actions. Quinnan rightfully points out how phrases such as "at-risk" marginalize students before they even set foot on campus. I once undertook a study of Native American college students on a "mainstream" campus where the admission counselor said that every Native American student was automatically placed in the "at-risk" category (Tierney, 1992). I have recently completed a work that points out the marginalization gay students and faculty face when they are looked on as "special interest groups" (Tierney, 1997a) rather than as full members of the academic community. Such language inevitably leads to policies and structures that divide communities. Similarly, in the text that follows we discover how adult students are marginalized by language, and thus by policies, in academic organizations.

Adult students are a compelling group to consider for two reasons. Usually adult students are first generation students, and of consequence, we are forced yet again to think about the implications of class with regard to education. The intersections of class are crucial for our understanding of who benefits and how we might change so that more benefit from educational institutions.

Further, adult students are the fastest growing group in academe. As Quinnan points out, close to sixty percent of current students in higher education are over the age of twenty-two. Surely we need to make sense of a majority who we continue to marginalize. Such a concern is of special importance at a time when academe moves toward radically different ways of delivering educational services (Tierney, 1997b). If we are to create greater equity and ensure that technological advances such as websites and listservs do not exist only for the elite, then we must understand those whom we serve. Higher education in the twenty-first century will be less that of "place"—a campus—and more that of interactions—personal, technological, and electronic. Accordingly, we need to come to terms with the cultural capital needed to succeed not only in the academic world of today, but also of tomorrow. In order to do so, we must comprehend the needs of those students who populate our campuses, and increasingly, they will be adult students.

Quinnan has opened a space for us to consider, debate, and discuss not only how we might better serve adult students, but also in doing so, how we might recreate communities for the twenty-first century that are more inclusive and at the same time, diverse, more willing to accept difference, and also create commonalities across divides. We come to learn yet again what it means when we think of individuals as "risks," and we consider the challenges that lie ahead for those of us who work in colleges and universities.

William G. Tierney
Los Angeles, California

REFERENCES

Tierney, William G. (1992). *Official Encouragement, Institutional Discouragement: Minorities in Academe—The Native American Experience.* Norwood, NJ: Ablex.

——— . (1997a). *Academic Outlaws: Queer Theory and Cultural Studies in the Academy.* Thousand Oaks, CA: Sage.

——— . (1997b). *The Responsive University: Restructuring for High Performance.* Baltimore, MD: Johns Hopkins University Press.

Acknowledgments

The true division of humanity is between those who live in light and those who live in darkness. Our aim must be to diminish the number of the latter and increase the number of the former. That is why we demand education and knowledge.

—Victor Hugo, *Les Miserables*

This acknowledgment is three years in the making—the time it took this book to grow from seed to harvest. To be sure, there were many moments along the way when I doubted it would ever see Hugo's "light." To continue to borrow his metaphor, there were indeed times I felt like the harried Jean Valjean, facing a parade of academic Javerts who pursued me with the goal of arresting the message of hope contained in these pages.

It is only through the almost constant support and persuasion of family and a few close colleagues that I prevailed in this undertaking. Foremost, I must thank Lela, my infinitely patient wife who put up with my absences for months when no one else would have. You know where you place on my list of extraordinary human beings. I would also like to express my gratitude to my two mentors during this project. Ed Wingard, without your unwavering faith in my "method of attack," this work would have withered on the vine of Academic Tradition. You also taught me how persistent pressure masked with a smile can ultimately win over even the fiercest critics—most of the time. I am also grateful for the friendship of Don O'Meara, a colleague at Raymond Walters College, who was as excited by postmodern interpretation as I was.

There were others who played key roles in keeping me focused by offering frank appraisals of portions of this manuscript. Merv Cadwallader—the kind of septuagenarian I hope to be someday—your recommendations for readings when I had lost all momentum turned out to be invaluable. Thanks, Tom Noyes, for a friendship that developed rather suddenly but stayed strong down the homestretch. Mareitta Alston, your humanity and its influence on me were gifts during the darker days of writing. Finally, my thanks to Celia Pritchard and Cindy Schmittauer, for their much-appreciated logistical and clerical help.

I will never underestimate the collective, positive force these people and their diverse talents exerted. You all helped to sustain me and this book during the last three years.

ADULT STUDENTS "AT-RISK"

Introduction

Demographics show that our population is continuing to grow older: birth rates are declining and longevity increasing. According to 1990 Census data, the median age of Americans today is 34.9; by the year 2010, it is projected to be 39 (*U.S. News and World Report*, August 21, 1995). This aging is altering the complexion of society and the institutions designed to serve it. Colleges and universities, paragons of the nation's educational system, are being looked to for leadership in preparing to meet the challenge.

This book is about adults who come to college. More precisely, it is concerned with understanding the culture of the university and how it affects the educational plans of mature individuals. Much of what the adult student encounters along the path to learning is not of his or her own making but is imposed by the academic culture. My analysis of the present state of the student-institution relationship may unsettle the reader because it advances a perspective that is rather unpopular in mainstream adult education research.

As teachers and administrators know but hesitate to admit publicly, much of the literature on the adult student experience in higher education strikes a prosaic chord. Studies are done repackaging hypotheses and reaffirming outcomes of earlier scholarship. This seems to be the uninspiring nature of adult education inquiry. A program implemented at one college soon sees replicas at a host of other institutions. Very little in the field of adult education resonates as innovative or daring. The widespread reluctance to seek fresh approaches to program leadership, blaze new pedagogical trails, or experiment with alternative philosophies is difficult to understand. Yet one meets it throughout the landscape of adult education research.

Overcoming this inertia is where this book breaks from the fold. The malaise of duplication will not afflict this study. A rehashing of old prescriptions for how adults can best be served will not dominate this narrative. Neither will one find impressionistic interventions or tired remedies that treat symptoms rather than root causes. What this author can deliver is a critically informed evaluation of the present state of formal adult education and academia's appalling dereliction in naming them cursory rather than substantive problems.

This investigation addresses political as well as educational issues. The commingling of authority, oppression, and resistance in determining who has power and who does not in adult higher education comprises the nexus of this examination. For until we leave behind dalliances on teaching styles or cocurricular activities to answer prime questions about empowerment and oppression, adult students will witness little change.

A penetrating look at America and the educational system supporting it reveals a darker dimension that the powerful among us prefer not to discuss. Higher education, assigned a premier role in helping us achieve equilibrium in matters of race relations, social justice, and economic parity, has a particularly unseemly side that works to undermine these democratic aims. In fact, contrary to public expectation, academia serves to replicate power structures, social relations, and capital privileges largely antagonistic to the common hope that education engenders equality.

Unfortunately, few methods of inquiry allow us to see beyond the polished veneer of academia and look into those recesses where investigation, however uncomfortable its initial findings, might do some good. To achieve that end, this study adopts the research methodology of theory, presenting an analysis based on critical and postmodern theories in order to appraise the undemocratic aspects of adult education as practiced in American colleges and universities.

Acknowledging this purpose, let me provide some explanation for this choice. William Tierney, a University of Southern California professor of education, offers a marvelous rationale:

To begin, critical theorists tie their investigations to a concern for social justice and democracy. Critical theorists work from the assumption that the world is marked by enormous suffering and injustice. Instead of trying to increase organizational effectiveness or neutrally describe the organizational world, the aim of critical theory is to understand the oppressive aspects of society so that those features may be transformed by those who are oppressed. (1991, p. 41)

As an analytical framework, critical theory asserts that through the socializing effects of family, state, and schools, the dominant culture is reproduced—hardly a revelation in itself. Critical theory, however, extends this proposition to argue that in the reproduction process the same centrist ideology, prejudices, and forms of hegemony encoded into our social fabric are also perpetuated. Historically, education has been used by the ruling classes to safeguard their power and privileges while simultaneously disempowering minorities: racial and ethnic groups, women, the elderly. To support this claim, critical theorists marshal an array of data appearing to substantiate that education reinforces the division of labor and therefore the class system by channeling different groups into different types of academic and career-training programs.

All is not lost, however. As a conceptual descendant of critical theory, postmodernism argues that education, properly reconfigured for transformative purposes, may still function as the great equalizer society wants to believe in. In viewing the college campus as a site of cultural struggle, postmodern educators can create learning conditions enabling a new consciousness to develop in students. This awakening will expose the ways and means of institutional oppression and in doing so arm students at a cultural disadvantage to spearhead the movement for emancipated educational environments.

In the following pages we will learn that one residual bias still tolerated, albeit quietly, in colleges and universities is that directed against mature students. Although persons twenty-two or older now comprise the majority of enrollments, their academic needs remain largely ignored. For so long a province of the young, the economically dependent, the obedient, higher education refuses to acknowledge its xenophobic culture and customs, especially as they inhibit accommodation for nontraditional, "new majority" students (Elliott, 1994).

Cultural adaptation, the only proven formula for change, is painfully slow in most large organizations, often occurring at nearly a glacial pace. Government and corporations are splendid examples of the difficulty of eradicating a "business as usual" attitude, even in moments of internal crisis. Amplify the intractability twofold and one begins to sense the recalcitrance of the academy. Perhaps because of a history dating back to the Middle Ages, universities took years to create their own cultural mystique and behavioral codes and still work hard to remain insulated from external interference.

But the years have passed, and academic attitudes concerning adult students that were acceptable a decade ago may have lost their currency. To stay in touch with the educational needs of an increasingly nontraditional clientele, habit must give way to invention. Before innovation can occur, however, we must systematically disassemble the machinery and defects of the old order so that a new one may be erected. This experience should prove liberating as we discard outdated notions of adult learning practice and let theory lift us to new heights. As A. R. Jonsen (1991, p. 15) metaphorically notes:

All theory results from the desire to escape from the crowding details of human business and to enjoy for a bit, the clear free air and sparkling light in which one can see all things together and with etched clarity. In that clear air, lowly maxims are transmuted into lofty laws. All theorists, I believe, feel that the higher you fly the more certain of where you are.

Aside from its poetic phrasing, the author's point is well taken; through theory alone can one construct a wider, holistic, and unsullied understanding of the object being considered.

In this book I propose to take the reader on a theoretical journey through several eras—premodern, modern, and postmodern—to illuminate genuine philosophical and organizational paradoxes in adult education. It is my belief that these contradictions categorically negate the possibility of education ever reaching its potential as an agent of emancipation. As it stands, such programs daily deny older students the chance to to acquire and nurture the critical reflection skills needed to transform society by granting their views a hearing in the classroom and affirming their experiences as a context for new learning. Of course, to get to this point one is presuming that society *ought* to be changed, a premise others might oppose. To them I would simply echo the words of those who detect desperate inconsistencies in the existing order: "It is a paradox of our times to see, within the same eye span, gleaming inner city high-rise hotels, office buildings, convention centers—and deteriorating schools and neighborhoods" (Parnell, 1990, pp. 103–104).

Can we honestly deny the sad truth contained in this painfully vivid image? If not, we are acknowledging that the present world leaves much to be desired and that human beings hardly exist in conditions conducive to growth, autonomy, and fulfillment. If the reader takes umbrage at the suggestion that our social, economic, and cultural arrangements are equitable and serve all Americans well, then she or he should find the coming discussion interesting.

Although a variety of approaches were considered in planning this study, none demonstrated the potential to transcend the frontiers of knowledge to the degree that theory does. It is, after all, in formulating new hypotheses for specific phenomena that we challenge and some-times extend the limits of accepted practice. I balked at the prospect of recycling past ideas and contemporary treatises in aspiring to accomplish much more. As acclaimed adult educator Patricia Cross (1981, p. 109) has reminded us: "One of the most underutilized vehicles for understanding various aspects of adult learning is theory."

To better understand adult education, critical theory and postmodernism will converge to form the research framework. Critical theories, including postmodernism and critical postmodernism, will revisit salient topics in adult education from a fresh perspective. This new vantage point will enable the reader to comprehend adult education in a seldom seen light, perhaps as it really is rather than what it professes to be. In doing so, contradictions and calumnies will sadly become visible. Yet these inconsistencies, unpleasant as they may be for educators to face, are necessary for metamorphosis. Transformation, after all, is neither authentic nor lasting until an honest admission of lingering injustices cleanses our practice.

In the following chapters, I present a detailed depiction of the areas where adult students are victimized by academic culture. Chapter 1 provides this study with two essential items—its research question and investigative methodology—both of which guide all subsequent discussions. The chapter introduces the reader to a new perspective on adult education through an integrated analytical framework of critical and postmodern theory. Chapter 2 defines the population, programs, and parameters of this study. It develops and contrasts the idea of adults "at-risk" against the backdrop of traditional definitions, arguing that cultural rather than cognitive factors are responsible for the phenomenon.

Chapter 3 takes a unique look at adult education for its economic implications. The analysis suggests that programs and services for older learners have been handicapped for a variety of economic reasons, most of which stem from institutional indifference in supporting adult learning endeavors. Chapter 4 describes a research study conducted by the author to field test the assumptions of critical theory with an adult student population. Chapter 5 explores "andragogy" as the instructional science for adults and its reformulation in postmodern terms. This chapter also presents an in-depth discussion of the postmodern condition, its antecedents, and implications for constructing adult learning programs. Chapter 6 considers an alternative leadership model for adult education, assuming that those currently in use are lacking critical components of vision for community, student empowerment, and leadership through service. The Postscript includes some final thoughts on the difficulties adult education faces and will continue to encounter in the future.

As we begin, I would like to extend an honest invitation to any potential reader who, after perusing this introduction or scanning the table of contents, is intrigued with the subject but unsure about proceeding. My theory-based orientation need not deter you: I have taken great care to ensure that this book is accessible. Like the subject itself and the research method that explores it, I intended this work to be inclusive, engaging teachers, administrators, students, and any other person concerned with democracy and justice in the practice of adult higher education. With that, I encourage you to read on.

Chapter 1

A Critical Analysis of Adult Higher Education: Research Question and Methods

In her lasting contribution to adult education scholarship, *Adults as Learners* (1981), Patricia Cross discusses the crucial need for theory to serve as anchoring for all our interventions. She cites the work of fellow educators who express similar concern over the lack of theoretical foundation in the field using phrases like a "conceptual desert" while another complains about the "debilitating" effects of theory-bereft practice. Lauding its relevance to real student issues, Cross summons adult educators to resume their theoretical work as an indispensable first step toward informed program planning and implementation.

The profession of adult education cannot advance beyond its present stage of development if one generation of adult educators simply passes on what it has learned through experience to the next generation . . . because each new generation of professionals simply catches up with the preceding generation rather than forging new frontiers of knowledge. The systematic accumulation of knowledge is essential for progress in any profession. In an applied profession, however, theory and practice must be constantly interactive. (p. 110)

Quite clearly, Cross makes a valid observation. New ideas and philosophies must be formulated and explored if the field is ever to evolve beyond its current boundaries. The objective is not to discredit or refute the value of previous work done in adult education. In functioning as a point of reference, such accreted knowledge acts as a base from which expeditions into uncharted theoretical regions may be launched. This work is one such foray as it seeks to expand the possibilities that critical theory and postmodernism project for an area of education that has remained relatively unchanged for years.

However, before any serious analysis of issues, it is imperative for the reader to grasp the specific concepts and assumptions of critical theories. This familiarization is all the more important because it will foster an understanding of the research paradigm directing this investigation. Note that in the above sentence I used the plural: critical theories. It is my conviction that adherence to a single mode of inquiry, even a broad theoretical one traversing disciplinary lines, invites scholarly myopia. No one construct can sufficiently elucidate the many facets of culture bias that adults face in higher education. Thus this study will integrate several perspectives, as each has singular strengths that permit fuller explanation of the object of analysis. As Jonsen (1991, p. 14) conjectures, justification for any research method "rarely comes from a single principle, but usually from the convergence of many considerations, each partially persuasive but together convincing with plausible probability."

I begin by describing the design of this study and how its structure promotes a progression allowing the development of a coherent theme on the endangered status of adult students in traditional higher education. Because I rejected a prescriptive, empirical methodology in favor of theory, abstract and concrete arguments must be systematically interwoven in a manner that tests the data generated. The second section describes and compares the three theoretical stances used in this project: critical theory, postmodernism, and, in true dialectical fashion, a synthesis of the two in critical postmodernism. This triad to discovery is neither unique nor novel. Other academics committed to transformative educational politics (Aronowitz and Giroux, 1991; Tierney, 1991, 1993) pioneered it with fruitful results in examining the primary educational crises present in our time. The resultant methodological matrix produces an incisive tool for discovery and one that prevents germane issues from escaping us. Additionally, the sequence of the narration parallels the history of these theories as we journey from premodern through postmodern times.

The next section discusses the interdisciplinarity of critical theories and their depth as credible empirical tools. The reader will learn more about their origins, nature, and applicability in exploring adult education philosophies and institutional practices. I believe that critical theories alone generate crucial insights that standard research design—by sidestepping the centrality of historical and political influences—does not (Kellner and Roderick, 1981).

The final portion of this chapter provides a critique of critical theory as a defensible medium of inquiry. As some of us have learned, radical theory has a way of galvanizing opposition in the academy. This reaction partly explains why it is seldom taught in graduate programs of education. Also, because many see it as threatening to the academic order, it is unfairly maligned as research by and for a malcontened fringe. Inhibiting as this is, dismissal of any challenge, imagined or tangible, to established structures of power is the university's customary response to dissent.

RESEARCH QUESTION

This study may bear both resemblance to and dissimilarity with a doctoral dissertation. This duality stems from its basis in theory rather than standard empirical design (pre-test, intervention, post-test, data analysis, conclusions). Given the study's aims, this stylistic duality is entirely acceptable. Clearly, we cannot reject out of hand all the precepts of research science and still retain scholarly credibility. Consequently, all the essential components of the qualitative model appear in these and the following pages: outlining the hypothesized problem which informs the framing of a valid research question, gathering and analysis of data, and discussion of implications.

On the other hand, these conventions will probably be the only guideposts familiar to many readers. By its nature, critical theories demand a radically different approach to the undertaking of research. Knowing that many research designs are politicized despite their pretensions of impartiality (Patton, 1990), critical theory declares its presuppositions up front. Little effort is made to array nonqualitative data and draw objective conclusions since a body of neutral knowledge does not, in fact, actually exist (Spring, 1988), nor does value-free research since the investigator is not free from personal or disciplinary preconceptions regarding the subject being studied (Lincoln, 1991). Knowledge is merely presented as objective by "knowledge brokers"— schools, teachers, testing agencies, or textbook publishers—whose authority and stature in the social order it safeguards.

More descriptively, this book will display wholeness as a connected series of essays on the adult experience in higher education from a distinct vantage point that only critical theory, postmodernism, and critical postmodernism can supply. Each essay could stand alone, as an article, and still make a contribution to the field. However, when read serially and cumulatively considered, the thesis of the work becomes that much more forceful. When viewed through the lens of critical theory, we gradually amass evidence that reality is socially constructed and hence modifiable through individual and collective will (Kothari, 1983).

This study seeks an answer to one overarching research question concerning adult higher education. Based on prevailing adult education philosophy and practices, are colleges and universities actually meeting the social and cultural expectations they claim to address? Extensive data gathered from the literature, reports on existing programs, and perceptions as recorded in the written accounts of adult students are ambiguous enough to suggest that a discontinuity exists between what formal adult education purports to offer and the dramatically different outcomes it achieves. In fact, in its first telling, the data appear to support the untenable position that academia, ostensibly an institutional champion of egalitarianism, marginalizes adult students through exclusionary beliefs and customs. Contrasting the philosophy of adult education against political realities portrayed in critical and postmodern representations, then, becomes our primary empirical task.

In choosing critical theory, this study unconditionally asserts that discrepancies in personal and subcultural power exist in society and its institutions, and seeks to expose the mechanisms used and contradictory messages sent by the dominant regime to perpetuate such inequity. Each of the essays in this volume treat different elements of the larger theme of marginalization, or systematic noninclusion, and how it impacts the status of adult students.

For scientific purists, this study may be viewed as tantamount to evaluation research. According to the *Handbook of Research Design and Social Measurement* (Miller, 1991, p. 7), the evaluation researcher "studies social processes to determine if a program or a project is accomplishing what it intends to accomplish." Though we need not apply too stringent an interpretation of this definition, it does impart an accurate impression of what I hope to accomplish in this book.

HISTORICAL CONTEXT OF MODERNISM AND POSTMODERNISM

The table accompanying the text summarizes the historical location of critical theories amid the conditions that bred them. In isolating the distinct features of modernist and postmodernist epochs, the reader will obtain a rudimentary but valid notion of this book's intermingled perspectives. It is important to distinguish these subtleties since postmodernism is not a summary rejection of modernism but instead involves a different iteration of its themes and ideas (Laclau, 1988). Critical postmodernism, per se, as a construct hypothesized by this author, is not constituted in a separate space since it traverses between modern and postmodern assumptions and extrapolates from properties of both.

Figure 1.1 presents a synopsis of the historical expressions of the modern and postmodern eras. This figure is not comprehensive, nor can it claim universality. In the fashion of postmodernists, after all, we must admit that there is no single avenue to truth, and the examples used for purposes of contrast might be very different if another educator outside the American experience prepared such a diagram. Still, it is highly instructive in displaying the prime motifs of each epoch. The taxonomy and some of the language were extrapolated from a table in Charles Fox's *Postmodern Public Administration* (1995), although major modifications have been made to elaborate on ideas omitted from his prototype.

What the chart may not make clear, however, is the location of critical theory in the continuum. As a product of twentieth-century pragmatism, critical theory is clearly anchored in modernism. Foremost, it is a theory derived from traditional social and economic sciences. Any serious consideration of its arguments requires grounding in the prominent academic teachings of Western thought. Working through critical theory's deductive methods and adherence to dialectical processes permits no less. Although the focus is on disputation and disavowal of Eurocentric "truth," which has resulted in some calling it "anti-Enlightenment" (Marcuse, 1989b), critical theory relies on the same rational processes to arrive at its conclusions—logic and deduction—as its more celebrated philosophical opposites such as positivism. Thus, while markedly different in the orientation of its propositions, critical theory assembles them with a methodology quite similar to other modernist humanities.

THEORETICAL INTRODUCTION AND DIALECTICAL INQUIRY

Let us spend a moment on the logic undergirding critical theory and its descendants. After all, its selection as this study's methodology was not random. What was it that attracted this author to it as a viable means to discovery?

Figure 1.1
Twentieth-century Epochal Ruptures, 1917–1945

- *World War I*
- *Russian Revolution*
- *Fascism*
- *Nazism*
- *Stalinism*
- *World War II*

	Modernism	Post Modernism
Economy	Factory, mass assembly, manual labor	Services, information, processing
Organization	Hierarchical, power-prescribed	Leveled, relationship/systems based
Politics	Democratic republics, majority rule (e.g., U.S. govt.)	Confederations, coalitional alliances, (e.g., European Economic Community)
Philosophy	Universal truths, elevation of reason metanarratives (great books)	Cultural relativism, elevation of desire, disparate texts-interpretations
Science (Methods)	Detached study, prescriptive empiricism, laboratory analysis	Invested study, ethnography, participant/field observation
Sociology	Assimilation, mainstreaming of difference, nuclear family	Fragmentation, multicultural expression, extended or single-parent family
Psychology	Authentic self, part of whole, "common good" as priority	Decentered ego, apart from society, "individual rights" priority
Entertainment	Print linearity, "serialization"— newspapers, books, films	Image montage, "moment in the life of," MTV, cyberspace
Education	Social reproduction, cultural transmission, institutionalized	Individual/group empowerment, cognitive differentiation, self-directed

Henry Giroux, an eminent critical theorist, enunciates the qualifications of critical theory for social science scholarship quite effectively:

The concept of critical theory refers to the nature of self-conscious critique and the need to develop a discourse of social transformation and emancipation that does not cling dogmatically to its own doctrinal assumptions. In other words, critical theory refers to both a "school of thought" and a process of critique. It points to a body of thought . . . in which the claims of any theory must be confronted with the distinction between the world it examines and portrays, and the world as it actually is. (1982, p. 9)

The "process of critique" Giroux mentions is the dialectic. Intentionally, dialectical inquiry uses ordered contrast as a means of highlighting difference, disjuncture, or adversity. In so functioning, it works to assist theorists in three distinct ways: (1) by exposing innate contradictions in an object/subject; (2) by fostering dialogue among divergent positions; and (3) by synthesizing solutions to discordant propositions.

Refined by the German philosopher G. W. Hegel (1912), dialectical reasoning takes the form of a syllogism: a statement (thesis) presumed factual is made. This elicits a counterstatement (antithesis) disputing the alleged fact. In turn, this leads the student to a reasoned outcome (synthesis) resolving the break between the two, or, minimally, averring that a dialectical reconciliation among them cannot be reached.

By way of illumination, let us use an erroneous but popular cultural myth concerning women. Its thesis would be that "women are the weaker sex" for a host of physiological and psychological reasons. Its antithesis would argue that women (not men) bear children, assume multiple and more difficult roles in society, and have longer life expectancy, thus refuting any attribution of "weakness." A synthesis, then, might contend that this common view of women is grossly misleading and self-contradictory, deducing that females, based on the counterclaims presented, may well be the "stronger" sex.

As a mode of critique, the dialectic works to uncover, through focused contrast, the self-negating properties of an object, institution, or belief. As Held (1980) notes, it reveals imperfection where wholeness is claimed, questions popular perceptions against actual realities, and, moreover, exhibits potentialities not yet realized. Therein lies the power of dialectic—exposing the internal dichotomy of an object or assumption and then theoretically reconstructing it along more logical terms.

Critical Theory

The common ancestor from which postmodernism and critical postmodernism descended, critical theory seeks to reveal the contradictory and hegemonic elements underlying our social and cultural arrangements (Freiberg, 1979; Fay, 1987; Bronner and Kellner, 1989; Ray, 1990). As a sociology, it can be both "enlightening and emancipatory by enabling individuals to become aware of the conflicting interests which shape their understanding and their lives" (Jones, 1988, p. 2). Moreover, it is premised on the belief that education should, according to its stated purposes, strengthen reasoning and interrogatory skills and in doing so act as a catalyst for personal empowerment.

According to Paulo Freire, the seminal figure in applying it to educational settings, critical theory's call is to confront, resist, and overcome the dominant ideology (status quo) through heightened consciousness of the many ways oppression is operationalized through institutional practices. Ideally, this burgeoning awareness will prompt mass reflective action, or praxis (Hart, 1990), precipitating dramatic change in the prevailing social system.

For Freire, a Brazilian teacher deeply troubled at how his people had been "colonised" (1973) in accepting the alien culture of the early Portuguese, education could not take the middle ground. If not liberating, it preempted social transformation by preserving predominant systems of power and control. More to the point, he saw the "purpose of education as an attempt to liberate adult students so they can take charge of their own lives" (Jones, 1988, p. 148) instead of serving as receptacles for an exported culture that reduced them to subordinate status.

Critical theory's lineage traces back to Marxism and therefore espouses elements of its economic tenets (Dickinson and Russell, 1986). Foremost among these is the notion that most injustice takes shape in the economic exploitation of the laboring classes by the wealthy. The ruling affluent achieve this by relegating much of society to unskilled occupations, limited economic advancement, fixed social position, and thus a disempowered existence. Educationally, this may be taken to mean that disadvantaged students of color or adults (as displaced laborers) are not ascribed the same native ability as traditional students. Thus they are often directed into abbreviated or technically oriented academic programs and consequently denied the same career and life choices majority students can expect.

The means of oppression are often embedded in cultural rituals and symbols we take for granted (Wolin, 1992), such as schooling and language. Critical theory therefore narrows the field in isolating the discrepancy between what is versus what ought to be—reality versus ideal—(Ray, 1990) in a democratic nation and the institutions (government, colleges, churches) pledged to serve it. Therefore, its analytical thrust comes in the exposure of contradiction and conflict. It is in the detection and demonstration of such paradox that this body of scholarship proves tireless.

A sterling example that critical theory supplies, by way of instruction, emerges from education's role as an agent of social reproduction (Bowles and Gintis, 1976). The theory of social reproduction has exerted far-reaching influence over educators since it first appeared in Bowles and Gintis' *Schooling in Capitalist America* (1976). In brief, the theory says that schools act to support the goals of the state. Oddly, conservative and liberals alike rallied around it, whether in efforts to improve the skills-training that education provides in raising the production capacity of the workforce (conservative), or to show the channeling of students from an early age into learning programs and ultimately occupations (liberal) that their economic origins imply. Critical theory contends that colleges, through overt and hidden means—methods of instruction (teacher as authority figure, lectures to disseminate knowledge), curricula (what subject is chosen and its presentation), and differential expectations or tracking practices (disadvantaged students being counseled into nonprofessional programs)—simply replicate the existing social system with all its divisions and inequities. In essence, these institutions are serving as vehicles of cultural transmission. Further, it stands to reason that the same values, norms, and biases inherent in the dominant ideology are reinforced during schooling and reproduced across generations with full approval of those in power (Bandyopadhyay, 1986).

Critical theory stresses the primacy of the collective (class, political party, economic caste) over the individual. In short, equality and justice are impossible in capitalistic society because wide economic disparity and resulting imbalances in power among social strata linger (Hearn, 1973). Finally, it is predicated on class solidarity as the only social verity and catalyst for mass transformation.

Postmodernism

Postmodernism offers a view of sociology moderately different from that of critical theory and picks up where the latter falters in addressing the social and educational dilemmas endemic to a postindustrial, transcultural world (Crook, 1992). In departing from critical theory's modernist roots, it replaces the integration of logic and reason with an outward momentum or psychology of fragmentation. Postmodernism celebrates differences and accentuates multivocality across public, cultural, and academic spheres (Tierney, 1993).

In postmodernism, rationalism and its treatises are replaced with diverse, discrete discourses, few of which may have any resemblance to the dominant regime's view of wisdom, morality, or science (Berube, 1994). It postulates the decentering of norms/self, deterritorializing public and political life to admit groups beyond the majority, and redrawing boundaries of knowledge and power (Aronowitz and Giroux, 1991) so that the "Other" avoids being pushed to the sidelines of civil discourse and acquires its legitimate voice in the exercise of democracy. "Otherness," a unique concept alluding to the cultural remoteness of any disadvantaged population (e.g., ethnic minorities, women, older persons), is crucial to the postmodern problematic.

Unlike critical theory, however, these other readings and voices are not met only in abstraction. In postmodernism, they are intended to be encountered, experienced, and lived. To do so, each of us must concede our own "politics of location" (Giroux, 1988a). By this, an admission is required from me that my status as a middleclass, educated, white male imbues me with a particular set of perceptions which I bring to my interactions with the world. Michael Awkward (1995) calls this one's "positionality" and contends that how successful we are in building multicultural communities depends on the degree to which we can learn alternate experiences of Otherness.

Another site of encounter for postmodernism is in the community. This theory posits that constructive social assemblies can be created despite the views of vastly differing groups as long as recognition of what constitutes acceptable thought and action is shifted away from the normative influence of majority culture (Stoll, 1994). In the postmodern landscape the notion of "norm" loses all potency in suggesting ideas and behaviors agreeable to the general population as widely consensual standards cannot be found across cultural formations (Richardson, 1991).

A subalternate theory focuses on "mediascape," or the realm of simulation, where class and culture struggles are now played out (Kellner, 1989). According to this theory, mass perception has been so distorted by the barrage of signs, pictures, and messages flooding us each day that an objective reality no longer exists. Economic and social tensions find release not in public discourse or participative politics but vicariously in the conflicts or ruptures displayed in music, advertisements, films, or television programs. Instead of the real, there is only the "hyperreal" (Baudrillard, 1988), a seductive netherworld where a herd mentality is induced and political and social vistas are purposefully crafted by culture-mediating industries.

Assuming that even some fragments of French postmodernism are valid, the search for enlightenment and meaning as encountered through educational institutions, already sites of cultural friction, becomes an extremely complex problem for contemporary academics.

Critical Postmodernism

Critical postmodernism is more than a melding of the previous theories. Here the notion of Otherness as distantly located evaporates as cultures are engaged in discussion and as decisions are made not through the will of the majority but through mediation of different and oftentimes angry (Hu-Dehart, 1995) voices on politically embroiled issues. Democratic dialogue, open and spirited, is in itself the transformative event (Agger, 1991) to be sought after.

To attain this breakthrough, understanding the solitude of otherness (Lorde, 1984)—in its particular pain and pride—is only the start. Finding a way to bridge the hostility and negotiate differences in establishing a just framework for interaction is paramount (Livingston and Berger, 1994). Here interpersonal relations are necessarily humane, cooperative, and growth-compelling. Most important, educational programs must be organized around one overriding principle: engagement. In addition, ideologies and behaviors are known to be relative to cultures they represent and so recognized by the critical educator, thus controlling for the possibility of hegemony in what is taught and how it is presented. Under these conditions, the Other's experience makes a meaningful contribution not only to their group but to the larger community which all subcultures must be committed to creating.

Finally, critical postmodernism returns us to familiar territory after probing the somewhat dogmatic frontiers of critical theory. Those issues underdeveloped in critical theory and postmodernism find a welcome place in this genre. If engagement is the apex of postmodernism, transcendence (Outka, 1972) becomes the goal of critical postmodernism. Here educators are not content with arresting exploitation (critical theory) and introducing expanded dialogue and action (postmodernism). What consumes most of critical postmodernism's energy is the naming and restoring of human variables—affect, desire, memory—into the analysis (Usher, 1994). Subjectivity, taboo in modernist rationalism but central to the body of postmodernism, is infused in the worldview of critical postmodernism, as it is pointless to explore educational possibilities in social and cultural terms yet ignore its human ramifications. Equally futile would be social research that begins with the omission of any and all grander considerations, such as the collective quest for social justice through education, and instead languishes in the common lore of a single subculture. In short, critical postmodernism envelops prominent themes of both contributing theories—modernism's logic and postmodernism's diversity—in reminding us that the need for answers must be balanced by compassion.

In borrowing a term coined by W. G. Tierney, critical postmodernism may be defined as a cultural politics of hope (1993, p. 22). Parsing this phrase for closer scrutiny, one discerns elements of critical theory and postmodernism incorporated into the gestalt of critical postmodernism. "Cultural" here is the inclusion of main and minority discourses and belief systems; "politics" affirms the knowledge-to-power link and how this relationship plays out in educational environments; and, finally, "hope" refers to the utopian future that critical postmodernism aspires to, despite extreme contrasts in our public and personal circumstances.

For adults, entering college with wonderfully diverse portfolios of life experiences and learning, critical postmodernism brings with it a multiplicity of approaches that could be used by educators to encourage the articulation and employment of individual student biography as supplementing formal instruction in the classroom.

INTERDISCIPLINARITY

Critical theory offers a perspective for apprehending the world in social and economic terms. As a method of inquiry, it is able to penetrate exteriors in revealing the true functions of social institutions as they reinforce the ideology and mores of the dominant culture (Smith, 1993).

Apart from noting and critiquing such phenomena, critical theory hopes to extend the limits of human potential by freeing persons from the machinery working to undermine their struggle for equality. Its contemporary cousin, postmodernism, broadens and updates these concepts by widening its philosophical stance to include and explain cultural diversity as the primary political flashpoint of the 1990s. Postmodernism also changes the focal point from class to culture (Outlaw, 1983) as the source of social unrest. Consequently, critical and postmodern science, in conjunction, offer the most appeal for those dedicated to restoring the theme of emancipation to the educational process.

To get there, critical theory bravely crosses disciplinary borders and liberally extrapolates from the humanities in forming a new sociology. Interdisciplinarity formed the core of critical theory since its nascence in 1923 at the Institute for Social Research in Frankfurt, Germany, out of the turbulent mists of the Weimar Republic. Max Horkheimer, co-founder and later director of "The Frankfurt School," as it came to be known historically, called for "a multidisciplinary integration of philosophy with the sciences in the hope of providing a theoretical instrument for transforming politics, society, the economy, and everyday life" (1972, p. 141).

Never a circle to shy away from challenge, Horkheimer's colleagues and protégés excelled in pursuing this legacy. The numerous works published by the Frankfurt School appropriated heavily from anthropology, history, economics, sociology, linguistics, and psychology. As you move through this study the fusion of these social sciences in developing our own critical project of adult learning should become eminently clear.

Similarly, the next generation of critical scholars picked up where the primogenitors left off. Bronner and Kellner (1989) give a contemporary rendering of critical theory's breadth:

Critical theory offers a multidisciplinary approach to society which combines perspectives drawn from political economy, sociology, cultural theory, philosophy, anthropology, and history. It thus overcomes the fragmentation endemic to established academic disciplines in order to address issues of broader interest. (p. 9)

Still, other academic luminaries in the past and present tradition of the Frankfurt School warn against the tendency of being swept away in the euphoria of forging an "interdisciplinary supertheory" (Kellner and

Roderick, 1981, p. 169) that may well be unattainable. However, transformative educators continue to believe that very few empirical models rival critical theory in addressing the totality of human social experience.

Perhaps the highest praise of critical theory as a microscope through which to view individual aspects as well as the macrocosm of society and its institutions comes from its mutability. The theory demonstrated a rare capacity for change in addressing the pressing issues of the day. Unlike other social sciences cemented in their infrastructures, this adaptability prevents critical theory from obsolescence. Also, it is forthcoming in owning up to its shortcomings and relies upon refor-mulation when its current readings fall short in analyzing contemporary crises. An advocate contends: "Inherently self-critical, it offers a well-articulated standpoint for thematizing social reality. . . . Against all relativistic and nihilistic excesses, critical theory seeks an emancipatory alternative to the existing order" (Bronner and Kellner, 1989, p. 2). Although critical theory and postmodernism have limitations as re-search methodologies, their insight in addressing a spectrum of social, economic, and cultural nuances and their desire to improve the political station of ascendant groups outweigh these weaknesses.

Emphasizing the transformative propensity of postmodern educa-tion, Canadian cultural anthropologist Peter McLaren avers, in *School-ing as a Ritual Performance* (1993), that to remain relevant, educational research must take on the qualitative aspects of ethnography, studying and writing about groups from their own sense of place, without straining out subjective factors such as rituals, symbols, and experiences in favor of hard data. To imagine critical scholarship as a multitextured approach to interdisciplinary study and a movement dedicated to liberation, yet articulated in a language sterilized of personal and social potentiality, is inconsistent. As a minority student recently ob-served to a colleague in deploring the college's official view of him as a demographic, "a story tells more than statistics could ever explain" (Stephens, 1993, p. 4).

METHODOLOGICAL VULNERABILITIES

No theoretical position is immune to criticism. If ever found to be impregnable, such a position would be hailed by scholars as the perfect science. Critical theory in its current incarnation continues to elicit protest from reactionary academic quarters (Bloom, 1987; Hirsch, 1987; Ellsworth, 1989) that prefer to treat academia as a cultural museum of sorts, a province to be defended against the crass onslaught of intellectual pluralism now menacing its frontiers.

In *Postmodern Education: Politics, Culture, and Social Criticism* (Aronowitz and Giroux, 1991, p. 59), even two of its staunchest proponents issue a reservation about blanket applications of critical theory and postmodernism without qualification. "Moreover, both discourses as forms of cultural criticism are flawed; they need to be examined for the ways in which each cancels out the worst dimensions of the other. They each contain elements of strengths, and educators have an opportunity to fashion a critical pedagogy that draws on the best insights of each." Hence the emergence of critical postmodernism in an effort to achieve just that.

I believe the alleged chinks in critical theory's armor that antagonists are swift to attack do not diminish its capacity to explain. As argued from the outset, the power of critical theory is its singular ability to examine educational topics from a vantage point that stresses the connection between knowledge, power, and social relations. Seeing that the claim of knowledge as neutral is a fallacy (Foucault, 1980), critical theory emphasizes the politics of education and redefines the field accordingly.

To its detractors, postmodernism surfaces as the latest vagary in theoretical trends. Critics claim it withers under field trial for lack of empirical roots and methodological rigor. For its part, postmodernism accuses social research design of being colored by the same conditions as the period and philosophy (Enlightenment, patriarchal, Eurocentric chauvinism) that bore them. With the ascendancy of border cultures, assaults on the pedigree of Western knowledge continue to mount in number and rancor. Postmodernism provides one forum for the waging of such ideological battles.

Moreover, certain schools (e.g., French) of postmodernism are excoriated as amoral, anarchical, doomsaying. This is particularly so for Baudrillard's (1994) "cyberblitz" musings and Lyotard's (1984) lamentations on the dissolution of meaning in our electronically hollowed-out world. Opponents contend that the French school's basic premise is unsound and therefore any conclusions drawn from such a theory of society cannot be trusted.

Still, hyperreality and what it conjures up by implication deserve a few moments' consideration. In such a place, ego weakness becomes the norm and individuality suddenly less enticing than deferring to the slogans and images saturating our computer monitors and television screens. Teleologically, this cyberworld presages social collapse as the culture industries (Adorno, 1967)—television and films, the media, and cyberspace—conspire to create a yawning black hole that drains the vitality of addicted masses who have surrendered to a fix of ever-increasing stimulation.

What this portends for educators is even more nightmarish: eroded intellects and attention-deficit students craving a similar bombardment of pictures and catchphrases in the classroom, none of which need be tied to the next or work linearly toward dénouement. While this scenario suffers from exaggeration, its precursors may be found in the stories teachers tell about the mounting problems they face in keeping students focused in the classroom. At a recent in-service retreat, faculty at the University of Cincinnati were told today's student displays an attention span of approximately "20 minutes" (Salvato, 1995, p. 7) after which the instructor must switch to another instructional method or risk losing students completely.

Apart from its rhetorical flair, postmodernism is also susceptible to criticism denouncing it as a "logic of disintegration" (Dews, 1987). If indeed modernist views of our social and political traditions have lost currency in describing the present world, what wisdom can be gleaned from postmodernism? On this count, its foes pinpoint a weakness. The radical project concentrates its analysis—like all leftist polemics—on negation, discrediting the authority of standard sciences, focusing on social conflicts and crises, and rethinking the altruism of institutions we were raised to trust in all our lives (Marcuse, 1963). Presuming they are successful in articulating what went amiss, what hope can they instill in educators bent on finding new cures for perennial dilemmas? At times, it seems, we are left groping for answers.

To be sure, traditional ideas cherished in both civic and private spheres are more or less swept away in the currents and eddies of critical theories. This is not all bad. For scholarship to deserve its name, it should judiciously scrutinize past assumptions about the nature of socially constructed and maintained systems. In this study, we are going one step further. Not only is higher education being examined for how it may have failed adult learners, but also redeemed in how it may yet find a way to do them justice.

ACADEMIC IMPERIALISM AND CRITICAL THEORY

Fierce resistance to the validity of critical theory arose during discussions in the planning of this book. Several colleagues consulted for the project raised doubts as to the legitimacy of critical theories as viable research methods. For them, imagining legitimate scholarship outside discipline-dictated paradigms was unthinkable. I would run up against this educational "logic of domination" (Aronowitz, 1988) and the ridicule accompanying it several times during the composition of this text.

Like many, these individuals, trained and steeped in Western intellectual traditions, had elevated the procedures of research to almost mythic proportions (McLaren, 1993). My proposal was probed, pricked, and dissected in the ensuing debate. How could one justify dialectic philosophy as a serious method of inquiry into adult higher education? What was its ancestry? What were its intellectual moorings? How could one hope to prepare an objective study of adults in higher education using a perspective thus predisposed? These were just some of the questions hurled at me.

It was not until after these conversations that I realized my first impressions were wrong. Initially, I wanted to believe my colleagues were unable to engage my thesis on a cognitive level. Their intentions were honorable, and they wanted to supply constructive criticism; it was simply an issue of subject matter foreign to them. It was only much later that I concluded it was not animosity toward the kernel of the book as much as mental rigidity and an unshakable sense of what constitutes acceptable research.

This study, as does most critical scholarship, required a conceptual loosening. Protests did not arise from unfamiliarity with the terminology or precepts. On the contrary, each challenger possessed an aptitude to grasp the issues. The problem did not lie in the questions being asked, nor was it the theoretical approach I suggested. Instead, it was my defiance in conceding to the primacy of academic research design. In short, standing against the dominant orthodoxy of empirical science was equated with heresy. Their indignation as "culture bearers" (Allaire and Firsirotu, 1984) was aggravated by my insult to the supremacy of this canon. Invisible to them, however, was how their devout defense of traditional models and practice promoted an authoritarianism of their own.

What remained unexamined in my predicament, and on a broader level, was the original contamination of the social scientific method by historically dated Eurocentrism (Apple, 1989). This research apparatus came in vogue during the eighteenth-century Enlightenment at the time when philosophes sought to lift reason above passion in world racked by religious and political strife. Thus the "scientific method" evolved from its own cultural context—an ideology biased toward

Western, chauvinistic, aristocratic influences. It is just as suffused with period/place values and referents as any endeavor involving humans automatically must be. Unfortunately, it hides this truth under a cultivated disguise of impartiality. Prophetically, this is precisely what postmodernism warns us against in fending off the imperialism of claims to universal texts and truths. Despite a centuries-old facade, "Western knowledge is encased in historical and institutional structures that both *privilege* and *exclude* particular readings, voices, aesthetics, authority, representations, and forms of sociality" (Giroux, 1992, p. 27).

The issue begging attention is why throughout the next two hundred years no one in the intellectual community challenged the legitimacy of this methodology. In *Leadership and the New Science* (1992, p. 121), Margaret Wheatley concurs and advocates a rethinking of our research designs along more contemporary lines:

We social scientists are trying hard to be conscientious, using methodologies and thought patterns of seventeenth century science, while scientists travelling away from us at the speed of light are moving into a universe that suggests entirely new ways of understanding. Just when social scientists seem to have gotten the science down and can construct strings of variables in impressive formulae, the (physical) scientists have left, plunging ahead into the vast "porridge of being" that describes a new reality.

Though the metaphor is picturesque, Wheatley captures the leitmotif of postmodernism in her "porridge of being." We do indeed need to look at things anew, as if walking out of the primeval forest and beholding them for the first time.

It is the inconsistencies in authoritative, prescriptive constructs and their complacency that critical theories are adept at combating. This project was challenged as being tainted from the start for its espousal of a theoretical stance sensitive to social and political concerns. Just as tinged, however, is the methodology my rankled colleagues were endorsing. Again, Wheatley suggests that scientific methods are so ingrained in our professional psychology that "we cannot escape their influence nor deny the images they have imprinted on our minds as the dominant thought structure of our society" (1992, pp. 141–142).

The academy finds many ways to bring its heritage to bear on coming generations of scholars through ceremonial and linguistic codes of cultural control (Cohen, 1993). The attempt to dismiss my research on grounds that it would be intrinsically flawed for choosing a unique methodology presents one such case. In their defense, my acquaintances were only reenacting a rite of passage from their own experiences in academic culture. I was not deterred, however, and this lesson proved most instructive and crystallized my decision to explore the adult experience in colleges and universities through the conceptual framework of critical theories.

EDUCATIONAL THEORIES OF HOPE

Critical theory and postmodernism hold allure not so much as theories of what has been lost as of what might be found in the statement of opposition and discourse of the Other. The hope of the critical project lay in this ambition: "For it is within the dialectic of oppression and transformation that the language of critique and possibility as the precondition for resistance can be learned and practiced in the context of everyday life. It is this interplay of history, memory, and solidarity that leaves history open" (Giroux, 1988a, p. xi). In turn, theory offers educators the freedom to evaluate thoughtfully and to affect the classroom and campus as sites of cultural contestation. In the end, these capacities redeem and raise critical research above the predictable patterns of traditional research. They also signify a fresh perspective on what otherwise appears to be a monotonous trend in adult education scholarship to tout old ideas as new findings.

Despite its political filter, critical theory is above all things concerned with human fulfillment and a society organized upon a morality of liberty and equality. In the sense that it declines to omit factors such as motive, affect, and aspiration as ingredients of its sociology, critical theories wander from the flock of academic methodologies. Even Delbert Miller, author of a monumental textbook on research design and measurement, concedes that in the "real world" scholarly methods are not immune to assorted social factors: "Causes and effects are hard to disentangle. In social science itself, many ideological differences reside in the very methodological approaches that are advised by various 'experts'" (1991, p. 5).

If his utterances and others like it are indicted as rebellion against the canon, critical theory pleads no contest. For far too long, the impetus to quantify our world and its living systems has become an end in itself rather than a means to an end. Almost thirty years ago Thomas Kuhn (1970), the renowned physicist, spoke of the pragmatists' refusal to let go of their academic training, knowing that outmoded scientific expectations live on long after facts that belie them have been brought to light. Kuhn attributed this obstinacy to the collective investment that faculty have made in a disciplinary paradigm, discredited or not.

Critical theories are not doctrines of despair in dismantling contemporary social formations and cultural meanings. On the contrary, they proceed from a kernel of hope. For its part, critical theory merely asks us to acknowledge the suppressive elements still alive in our society. And, much like the phoenix's rise from the ashes in classic myth, postmodernism emerges as the new sociology while former sciences surrendered their ability to remain relevant.

Finally, critical postmodernism envisions a postprejudicial world of infinite possibilities where educational communities arise from celebration of difference and dissent, being particularly amenable to the sundry biographies and experiences of adult students as they lend an aesthetic richness to the process of learning.

Chapter 2

Adult Students "At-Risk": Theoretical Definitions

As we embark on our discussion a profile of the students served by this project is necessary. As hypothesized in our research question, adult learners may be at cultural risk in university settings. Before presenting a case for their endangerment, this study must start by delineating the affected group. Additionally, gaining a better understanding of the social stigma "at-risk" carries, as well as exploring the circumstances surrounding how it came to envelop adults, requires our early attention.

After exploring these and attendant cultural expectations thrust upon mature learners by the academy, I will discuss how adults, unfairly bestowed with "at-risk" standing, are yet another variety of Other—besieged groups struggling to secure their own cultural niche on campuses largely indifferent to multicultural presences and needs (Montero, 1995). To be successful in clarifying this study's population and parameters, two initial tasks must be accomplished in this chapter. First, I will seek to establish a link between traditional, cognitive notions of "at-risk" and the project's view of this phenomenon in cultural terms. Second, I will examine how critical and postmodern theory might project adult learners to be a previously unnamed variety of "Other" and "at-risk" on that count. Finally, I hope to make clear the impropriety of perceptions of "at-risk" as *organically* insinuated. Many students so labeled spend their entire academic lives trying to undo the perception that something is naturally absent from their physiology, psychology, or personality. This is a desperately flawed assumption in that social contributions to the determination of "at-risk" status are patently ignored. Adult students, exiled to the fringes of academic culture, stand as testimony to what is wrong with the logic of "at-risk."

OUR "ADULT" STUDENT AND INSTITUTIONS INCLUDED

The term *adult student* is used somewhat freely in this study. Generally, it is intended to encompass all learners enrolled in postsecondary institutions who fall outside the 18–21 year-old age range. Of necessity, then, our study cohort includes any student whose age exceeds the high end of these parameters.

The Chronicle of Higher Education *Almanac Issue* (1996) survey indicated that in the fall of 1993, 58.2% of all (full and part-time) college and university students were 22 or older. At community colleges this cohort was 40.6.% of full-time enrollment, while at comprehensive colleges this figure was 30.9%. Alone, this data may elicit a raised eyebrow but does not tell us much more than most educators already know: adults are a growing segment of the campus population. Information compiled by the National Center for Education Statistics (NCES) and reported in the National University Continuing Educators Association (NUCEA, 1995) newsletter, however, will meet with greater surprise. Over the twenty-year period 1971–1991, the enrollments of students age 25 or older showed a meteoric rise, increasing by 171%. Within this pool, some other striking patterns emerged: ages 25–29 saw a 99% increase, 30–34 a 201% rise, and the 35+ cohort a 248% increase in representation.

Premature as it may be to generalize, one may still draw several conclusions from these figures. First, adults are rapidly becoming, and in many instances already are, the predominant age set on American college campuses. Second, the NUCEA-reported rise in the 30+ and older group suggests that career motives are behind the enrollment bulge. Job displacement, divorce, single-parenting, skills updating as it helps secure income for the family, all are possible factors for the surge in adult student enrollment. Last, the sheer percentages reflected in the NCES/NUCEA data are astonishing in spite of being a few years old. It would be intriguing to examine how much more adult proportions of student enrollment have grown during the period since the study was completed. By any stretch, these trends necessitate change in the way higher education conducts its affairs.

The academic institutions upon which I will focus include four-year, graduate and research universities. Narrowing the scope further, they will be those located in the United States. This way, we can be secure in our knowledge of the ancestry and customs of the organizations, programs, and perceptions that will be analyzed in subsequent sections.

With their long open-access history, community colleges are not as culpable as other postsecondary institutions in erecting barriers and are therefore exempted from this study. The case has even been made (Kempner, 1991) that community colleges, because of their long-standing role as educational servers of nontraditional students, have been relegated to the same academic Siberia as the multicultural clienteles that populate them. If so, such bias would partly explain why denizens of the ivory tower continue to deride community colleges as inferior. As 1993 data indicated, 77% of part-time and 40.6% of full-time enrollments at two-year colleges were students 22 years of age and older (Chronicle of Higher Education, 1996, p. 17). Nonetheless, it would behoove faculty and administrators in community colleges to retain a keen interest in the national predicament of adult students—if for no other reason, to increase awareness of where fellow institutions are failing and work to supply them with sufficient information for planning alternative program responses.

Yet we are not so restrictive in our definition as to omit older students who rely, at least partially, on supplemental monetary assistance from parents or family. To exclude them would mean the loss of many single mothers and fathers who, in addition to being students, are working part-time and depend on relatives for day care or household management while at work. Given the sometimes massive obstacles to completing education plans, their stories are especially instructive in documenting the barriers adults surmount. Their struggles will be recounted in more detail in Chapter 4.

Worsening an already untenable position, adult students may well be "at-risk" on more than one count. Age is the primary factor; gender is the second. In 1993 women accounted for 55% of the total enrollment in higher education. In community colleges where nontraditional students tend to be the norm, 61.3% of reported part-time enrollments were female. Considering the implications of these figures alongside the data presented earlier, it is reasonably safe to state that a significant percentage of adult students are in fact women.

Am I suggesting that a correlation exists between age, sex and subordinate status at the university? Unequivocally, yes. In future analyses we will see that marginalization does not selectively discriminate among assorted attributes of Otherness. The "isms"—sexism, racism, ageism, classism—are ubiquitous in the academy and in combination can prove culturally lethal for the nontraditional student (Welton, 1993). To be sure, being an older student does not automatically mean the indignities suffered are any more acutely felt than what other minority traits evoke. When these traits of Otherness converge, however, the perceptible level of opposition is certain to intensify.

DEFINING "AT-RISK"

The term *"at-risk"* conjures up much discussion across the pedagogical landscape. The phrase is customarily tied to secondary schooling in the United states but is nonetheless familiar in the terminology of college and university as well as K-12 educators. Lawrence Gold, president of a Washington-based educational lobby specializing in nontraditional student policy advising, unfortunately speaks for many in higher education when compressing the issue of "at-risk" adults into "people whose lack of education and training leave them unable to function in the job market" (Gold, 1992, p. 33). In their estimation, adults are not in peril because of academic weakness but rather because of their economic unfitness. This widely adhered to belief of adult education as inextricably linked to economic advancement is a fallacy doing students and colleges great harm by persuading both that education, as training for work, is the *only* worthwhile objective in adult programs (Cervero, 1988). Adult education and its career ramifications are more fully explored in the next chapter.

To pedagogues, "at-risk" suggests students who are in danger of failing to succeed, that is, in danger of failing to pass required courses and navigate the prescribed curriculum. Cognitive and emotional deficiencies are typically cited as causes for underachievement. Class and culture biases replete in the schooling process have been raised as factors contributing to the "at-risk" equation (Richardson, 1991) but seldom receive more than nominal treatment in discussions among educators. Currently, students so "flagged" by placement tests at the time of entry get channeled into special preparatory programs identifying them before their peers as different and, let us say it, inferior. In consequence, these students are further stigmatized with the labels of "remedial," "developmental," or "challenged." Moreover, the social and economic variables shaping the student's past are at best accorded a minimal role in rendering them susceptible to discrimination (Nieto, 1992).

Conventional wisdom, if at all trustworthy, usually implies "at-risk" clientele face obstructions to learning in the present because of past shortcomings in their preparation. The usual example is the inner-city student who attended a series of ill-equipped public schools (Payne, 1984). His teachers were poorly trained, auxiliary resources (tutors, labs, computers) scarce, truancy and related misbehavior unchecked, and the diversion of drugs and deprivations of poverty ever present. Though this example is exaggerated, it conveys certain insights.

For higher educators, another version of "at-risk" emerges in the plight of the returning adult student, who is also greeted by lower academic expectations and fewer institutional resources. In some instances it may be the woman who puts off seeking a degree for marriage, to have children, to raise a family and now, facing a midlife divorce and the exigency of supporting herself, decides to chart a new life course. Just as easily, it may be the mid-career male ousted during the last round of corporate restructuring who, in order to be competitive in a highly technical job market, urgently needs to update his skills and knowledge base (Simmons, 1995).

The binding thread between the two, one might argue, lies in the fact that both the K-12 "at-risk" case and adult students are poorly equipped to perform up to academic standards. The primary difference is where the doubts about success originate: adult students are hampered by self-imposed doubts (Apps, 1981) while pre-college students may more often be hindered by external forces outside their making or control. In searching to allay such anxieties, adults meet and yield to an internal impulse to address inadequacies (Knowles, 1984), while the adolescent, without the life experience to produce a similar awareness, finds this insight elusive.

The cause of "at-risk" status, per se, whether poverty-induced as was the case with the urban youth or merely postponed for domestic reasons like the adult, is secondary. Neither student is destined to excel because they lack something in their scholastic backgrounds. However, the disadvantaged status put upon adult learners by universities designed to serve a younger population is somewhat mitigated by the adults' intense inner drive to prevail (Stephens, 1993). Positive self-concept and the need to grow, which education should support and encourage, are crucial to overcoming the "at-risk" stereotype.

Administrators put a slightly different spin on the idea of "at-risk." For them the problem revolves around nonacademic hurdles to reaching educational goals (Stoll, 1994). Among this set of obstacles, support service shortcomings are key factors in adult attrition: weak financial aid packages, shortage of day-care facilities, irregular advising opportunities, or inflexible course scheduling (Wingard, 1995). These barriers may indeed exert a dampening effect on the enthusiasm of adult learners and undercut their academic plans by making the campus appear an unfriendly, even hostile place. In conjunction, pedagogical and organizational inflexibility (Parnell, 1990), creating an ambiance of indifference to adult students, increases the chance of their discontinuance. However, in this schematic, the root causes of marginalization are shifted from organic or native inadequacy in the student to cultural bias in the host university. This proposition marks a departure from traditional discussions and directs the reader along a path into new theoretical terrain.

CRITICAL AND POSTMODERN THEORIES' VIEW OF "AT-RISK"

Critical theory studies the cycle of oppression. Averring, prima facie, that differences in personal and group power precipitate unjust social arrangements (Aronowitz, 1981), it concerns itself with the ways and means of repression since they are typically concealed in the larger tissue of organizational and social formations. Conceptually, critical theory claims it is inconceivable to view individuals existing in capitalist nations apart from their economic usefulness to society and, in turn, their capacity to be exploited by the powerful for purposes of production. In corollary, then, it proposes that the most likely candidates for disempowerment are those lowest in the economic hierarchy (Navarro, 1979), as they lack the cultural capital—property, wealth, or knowledge—to be politically reckoned with. Taking this to its logical conclusion, those at the greatest disadvantage in our society tend to be the least affluent: minorities, women, the elderly, or for that matter, the chronically unemployed. Critical theory disassembles these culturally constructed views on production for their impoverishing and oppressive elements.

Adults, when assuming the role of students, as we will see in the next chapter, bear the same social burden as other marginal groups. A culture as driven as ours by capitalism and the puritan work ethic, regardless of how these concepts have been adopted and transmitted by higher education institutions (Veysey, 1965), still refuses to tolerate those who fail to abide by norms so embedded in our social fabric. To some, adults as students are an affront to American democracy—where corporate and government leaders collude to promote commercial interests at the expense of other priorities such as social justice and economic equality (Marcuse, 1989c). It is from these normative grounds—the fact that adult students are defying a solemn social obligation in choosing school over work—that deeply rooted cultural opposition to their inclusion in campus life springs.

Postmodernism, as an extension of and, in certain conceptual areas, a break from critical theory, addresses the difficulties adults enrolled in higher education face in markedly different terms. Economic issues are not as central to postmodern theory. The emphasis here lies on the cultural rather than the class hegemony (Tierney, 1991) that persons face in relation to society. Adult students, as a burgeoning but politically naive cohort in the larger educational landscape, form a distinct cultural association all their own. And, like other groups distinct from the center, the adult student collective is seen as subordinate to the main.

Postmodernism then places the question of representation before us. If indeed adults comprise a new subculture in the extremely rigid, change-resistant environment that is academe, are their voices, perspectives, and experiences assigned value similar to the dominant group? Or are they, as this theory anticipates, equated with Otherness (Giroux, 1990), a nameless, faceless attribute forced upon disadvantaged groups different from the majority because of race, ethnicity, gender, class, or age? In this conviction, postmodernism is unrepentant: despite social and institutional promises of embracing multiculturalism—alternative truths and different tellings—reality shows that a politics of exclusion (Reid, 1995) continues to hold sway.

As a result, adults quickly learn that universities welcome them as long as their usual ways of operating do not have to make accommodation (Riessman, 1980). Where older students find the going becomes more treacherous is in raising challenges to bureaucratic structures and attitudes designed for younger, less sophisticated counterparts. With life experience in testing boundaries, adults are a potential threat to the authority and autonomy of the academy by virtue of their unwillingness to abide by the status quo (Karol and Ginsburg, 1980). Because they use this experience base critically to assess course content, college policies, and teaching styles, adults place themselves at further risk in higher education for challenging not just the authority of the academy, but the values and beliefs—or ideology—undergirding university culture (Paterson, 1979). In traditional academic cliques, adults may be viewed as invaders into the body politic (Boyer, 1990), bringing with them demands that could prove an anathema to the power and prestige of those nestled safely in the academy. In postmodern theory, adults earn "at-risk" status simply because they are culturally suspect to the established order. Like other nontraditional populations, their increasing numbers on campus also guarantee a greater influence in shaping institutional practices affecting their learning (O'Connor, 1994).

THE CONCEPT OF CULTURE AND "BORDERLANDS"

Our inquiry necessitates a brief consideration of *culture* as a point of embarkation into our narrative. For purposes of this essay, the reader must discard popular notions of what culture entails. In this treatment, culture will not be abridged to impressionistic terms. It declines to be dictated demographically through pigmentation, ethnic indicators, or per capita income. New ways of looking at culture and its supremacist leanings evolve from the body of critical theory and postmodernism (Aronowitz and Giroux, 1991). More often than not, "culture" is used in discussions as a summons to communality, puportedly bringing diverse groups to an understanding of what is important in their collective heritage. Yet critical theory reveals the undemocratic propensity of culture, as manipulated by the dominant regime, in how it acts to silence or exclude certain peoples. The frames of reference these conceptual schema provide are both incisive and disquieting in uncovering the controlling aspects of culture.

Herein, "culture" denotes the representation of a specific social experience and epistemology (way of making meaning) in time. It may be perceived through a preferred set of processes (behavioral and cognitive), symbols (stated and intuited), and a discourse (language for meaning) (Habermas, 1987, 1992) permitting the group to arrive at a center of separateness, of self-awareness, apart from the social whole. The flowering of African-American urban communities as a highly indigenous embodiment of culture demonstrates this point. For many removed from it, the vernacular, actions, and worldview of its members are difficult to apprehend. The rise and persistence of rap music as an encoded medium of expression within this subculture is a another illustration.

As shown with rap music, these cultural processes and symbols often display opaqueness and protect against intrusion from beyond the boundaries of the group. Thus culture may be summarized as the realization of collective identity and communality of expression that bind persons together. Subculturally, it is the edification and rehearsal of patterns of being, articulated and metaphoric (McLaren, 1993), distinct to a populace but generally unknown across the wider social landscape.

As one might guess, higher education functions to preserve the dominant culture and enervate subcultures under the pretext of teaching a Western, liberal curriculum. The dispersion of disadvantaged student populations to regions beyond the staked territory of the academic majority is the result. Fluent in the dominant culture's language and practices yet never actually part of it, these students traverse daily between its boundaries and those of the discrete zones they inhabit (Hicks, 1988). To survive, these Others must plot a location in both the dominant and peripheral culture, the first dictating their station in society and the second providing a distant cultural axis around which personal spaces are hewn and connected to others in their association.

In *Border Crossings* (1992, p. 30), critical theorist Henry Giroux paints a more vivid picture of these borderlands:

These are not only physical borders, they are cultural borders historically constructed and socially organized within rules and regulations that limit and enable particular identities, individual capacities, and social forms. . . . The terrain of learning becomes inextricably linked to the shifting parameters of place, identity, history, and power.

Not content with merely recognizing their existence, transformative educators are excited by the learning potential these borderlands contain in extending our educational frontiers. They "represent a space in which to re-theorize, locate, and address the possibilities for a new politics based on the construction of new identities, zones of cultural difference, and forms of ethical address" (p. 28). Other critical and postmodern theorists sketch out related aspects of these borderlands. In *Borderlands: La Frontera* (1987), Latina author Gloria Anzuldua expands on these zones and their shifting membranes: "A borderland is a vague and undetermined place created by the emotional residue of an unnatural boundary" (p. 3). The "unnatural boundary" she speaks of alludes to its origins which are cultural, intangible, and therefore largely permeable. Tierney (1993, p. 7) describes these spaces with an economy of words, simply stating that "Border zones are cultural areas infused with differences." Just as Istanbul, Hong Kong, or Tijuana provide geographic sites where diverse people, traditions, and values meet and sometimes clash, educational border zones exist at the crossroads of different cultures and contextualize the exchanges of information that occur within them. As students, adults become Others by residing in a borderland between the college's main and subordinate cultures. Consonant with other border cultures, however, the adult learning community's discourse is vibrant and its history ready to unfold before those who are interested in its telling.

ADULTS AND OTHERNESS

If I have capably argued that cultural rather than academic barriers may be the culprits behind the problem, where does that leave us? Although a large question, the inklings of a solution are present in theory. Certainly, we break ranks with the powerful professsorial enclave who "ruthlessly deny" or culturally disparage the humanity of difference, of Otherness (Giroux, 1992, p. 33). After all, marginalization cannot be reduced to a purely political syndrome once its antecedents are recognized. The strategic omission of the discourses of the underprivileged appears far too frequently in our history for such an assumption. It must be, as commanded by critical theory, deconstructed into finer strands. These strands are threaded through an interpretation of "at risk" in postmodern logic, including its mooring in the concept of Otherness.

bell hooks, an African-American feminist and provocative thinker, provides an understated yet image-rich impression of Otherness in recounting her own youth in a small southern town:

Living as we did—on the edge—we developed a particular way of seeing reality. We looked both from the outside in and from the inside out. . . . Our survival depended on an ongoing public awareness of the separation between the margin and the center and an ongoing private acknowledgement that we were a necessary, vital part of that whole. (1984, p. i)

The feeling of estrangement suffusing this passage is shared by all individuals living on the edges. As we will see in the chapters ahead, adult students encounter similar feelings as they are forced to play roles of Otherness on many campuses.

Yet in the midst of this separation, a longing for reunion with the center, to become "part of that whole" comes through. It is this poignancy in being torn between cultures, situated in the personal and familiar but pulled, through schooling and public life, toward the social, that the essence of Otherness finds expression. In *Sister Outsider*, Audra Lorde (1984, p. 112) echoes:

those of us who are poor, who are lesbians, who are Black, who are older— know that *survival is not an academic skill* [italics added]. It is learning how to stand alone, unpopular and sometimes reviled, and how to make common cause with those others identified as outside the structures in order to define and seek a world in which we can all flourish.

In abstraction, Otherness has been theoretically projected as the "politics of location" (Giroux, 1988b). To grasp fully the experience of Otherness, one must acknowledge the culturally imposed attributes of his or her existence as they decide one's apprehension of experience. For instance, each of us cannot ignore the fact that our social status is largely determined by personal characteristics. In my case, the panoply of traits include being white, male, of European descent, educated, and middleclass. In composite, these factors coalesce to shape my value system, a set of beliefs, an ideology unique to me. Extending this phenomena to the cognitive domain, I subsequently adopt a perceptual filter derived from the confluence of these variables that creates and dominates my view of self, society, and world. Awkward (1995) alludes to the process of comprehending and owning up to this plotting of one's political constitution as *positionality*. How successful we eventually are in establishing multicultural communities depends on the degree to which we all concede our positionality, accede the predispositions it incurs in coloring our worldview, and strive to see beyond it in enabling us to encounter Otherness on terms not dictated by cultural mores.

Postmodernism's embrace of Otherness brings added theoretical depth to our consideration of adults "at-risk." As astutely noted (Aronowitz and Giroux, 1991, p. 188), it rejects broad brush approaches "that view the Other as deficit." Postmodernism endorses a critical yet compassionate educational "practice in which voices and traditions exist and flourish to the degree that they listen to the voices of Others, (and) engage in an ongoing attempt to eliminate forms of subjective and objective suffering" (p. 189) in remaking the college into a radically democratic community. Optimally, this community would be democratic enough to provide room for all students mindless of age, race, or gender.

Precisely how "radical" any social formation is that treats all its membership as autonomous and gives them equal rather than unequal voice (Marcus and Tar, 1984) is left to the judgment of the reader. I believe a tragic indictment of late capitalism is lodged in asserting that something so elementary in democratic principle must be regarded as "radical" for professing such a basic conviction.

Nor can we avoid the politics of precariousness affecting the adult student. Pedagogical and organizational models require transformation to reflect a diffusion of power as we move from vertical (hierarchical) to horizontal (participatory) educational paradigms. Instructional methods, bureaucratic systems, and faculty perceptions must also metamorphose into more collaborative leadership and faciliatative styles if higher education is to retain efficacy in the mosaic society of the twenty-first century.

Another way to alleviate the "at-risk" condition of adults is in the introduction of alternative teaching models such as the "andragogy" of Malcolm Knowles. Postmodernism, as a multifaceted theory of cultural criticism (Wolin, 1992), adapts and proposes a variation of educational method in its offering of border pedagogy. Border pedagogy (Giroux, 1992) will become the new science in training the next generation of faculty. Teachers will learn to serve as critical guides to students evolving their own sense of place in historical, cultural, and social contexts. Students will also be persuaded to explore the tensions and contradictions in personal experiences not as a means to discredit them but instead to examine their inherent political dimensions. Again, a vision for this future is provided: "Of course, it is crucial that critical educators provide the pedagogical conditions for students to give voice to how their past and present experiences place them within existing relations of domination and resistance" (p. 131).

This is particularly important for adult students who have accrued a lifetime of experiences which are affirmed by professors as integral to learning and made a regular part of classroom fare. Once the teacher enables self-narrative to develop, the prospect of a learning dialogue (Livingston and Berger, 1994), wherein students contribute from a position of elevated personal status, arises. Under such instructional conditions, the adult assumes new responsibility for his/her own learning. In taking control, s/he revises the terms of the contract with the academic institution and emerges in less danger of alienation from the educational process. In sum, then, it follows that the student's "at-risk" status diminishes dramatically after the cultural and political terrain of the classroom has been collectively explored and remapped. These and related issues will be treated in greater depth in Chapter 5.

MARGINALIZATION AS A CULTURAL OUTCOME

For its part, academic institutions deny the adult's quest for educational cure by deploying an army of ritualistic barriers through which the "new majority" (Elliott, 1994) must acculturate or face censure. So interpreted, "at-risk" could be taken as success or failure in the student's initiation into academic culture.

When placed in a cultural context, this "at-risk" condition is more properly understood as marginalization. Williams (1992) explains marginalization as living the minority experience with an awareness that escape from it is impossible. It is inescapable because marginalization denotes the systematic exclusion from full and equal participation in civic, economic, and political spheres of life. Further, marginalization brings a sentence of permanent disempowerment with society's broader consent. Members of marginal groups see, feel, and interact with the dominant culture in daily encounters yet sense their total powerlessness to alter it. Despite the toll of alienation, Williams argues that there is still "significant learning power inherent, not in deprivation, but in marginality" (p. 45) since those in its grasp are forged in crucibles of struggle. Ascendant groups then turn to education as a liberating force in kindling hope for a future without oppression. We will later examine how the experience of marginality can be broken down and reconstructed into a motivational agent for adult students and teachers.

Still, adults are imperiled when set against the backdrop of academic culture (Tisdell, 1993a). Resistance to it may be the single most important determinant of whether they are absolved of marginal status or whether it persists in plaguing them. Further, the threat that adults portend is more imagined than authentic. Where an adult presence in the classroom, the dean's office, or the boardroom could signify an injection of vitality into a somewhat complacent educational enterprise, it is more frequently regarded as a threat to the established power structure. In response, academic apologists dust off and polish an array of arguments in shoring up the university's defenses against the rising tide of andragogical (the science of teaching adults) and other student empowerment movements (Holford, 1995).

Why? Mature learners may challenge faculty used to monologic lecturing of passive adolescents from the great books of Western authors long revered as cultural luminaries. They might trouble administrators unaccustomed to explaining the logic of why blanket policies ineffectual at addressing the needs of working student-parents exist in spite of irrelevance. They could demand swift rather than prolonged change in an institution that believes its own myth about itself as a privileged, largely ceremonial community secluded from the world. They might hasten the encroachment of social accountability from an increasingly wary polity, and in the process watch faculty autonomy erode. For much of the old guard, these vistas inspire fear and indignation.

Ultimately, the key issue is acquiescence to university codes, practices, and behaviors (Heaney, 1993). Dissent is difficult for the academy to digest when it occurs outside the closed precincts of faculty meetings or administrative retreats. Academics are stalwart defenders of intellectual freedom *within* their own professional elite (Horkheimer, 1974). When challenged in quarters outside these venues, tolerance quickly evaporates. Open and critical debate, the philosophical foundation of university life, seems to be more fiction than fact when sought beyond the tenured rank and file.

Given the historical entrenchment of this culture bias, older learners remain vulnerable to expulsion from the intellectual Eden that conservative quarters in the university still fight to preserve. Esoteric ideals and trappings, few of which have currency in the multicultural, postmodern here-and-now, die hard. And dissent, the cornerstone of academic freedom, serves to protect the privileges of the old guard more than guarantee the free speech of "leftist" students or teachers. A scholar made the following discovery as an outspoken intellectual caught in the cultural machinery of the university:

I made the mistake of thinking that all major universities generally provided a setting where a critical dialogue could be constructed, oppositional views aired, or for that matter, where alternative positions could be taught. It now appears there are very few universities left in the United States where . . . freedom is taken seriously. (Giroux, 1982, p. xii)

Indeed at times, as Giroux laments, the "script is grim" and unlikely to recast the power of "academic assassins who act without compassion or reflection" (p. xii) in quelling dissent.

ADULT EDUCATION VERSUS ADULT LEARNING

In this our definitions chapter, we need to clarify precisely what type of educational programs we are investigating. Conversely, by selecting these parameters, we necessarily determine which programs do not concern us.

Although the phrases *adult education* and *adult learning* are considered synonymous and used interchangeably, in fact they represent two discrete entities. *Adult education* encompasses institutionally based (Jarvis, 1987b), structured educational interventions an older student encounters in attending college. *Adult learning* embraces the process of developing new knowledge, awareness, and skills across the span of life situations both beyond and within academic environs. The first is preoccupied with understanding the impact of the organization on adults, while the latter focuses on the processes, primarily informal and met across life's terrain, of knowledge apprehension. Although adult education cannot preclude learning, it must be noted that the two are separate, though often intertwined, processes.

Lest the reader be uncertain, this book concentrates on adult education as it has been and is formally practiced in American colleges and universities. The cognitive phenomena of (adult) learning are matters left to psychologists. The focus here is on the structures, concepts, and techniques predominating in organized academic systems. Further, if sociocultural factors help determine whether adults are going to succeed in institutions, it is important to differentiate between education and learning, as the two vary widely in the means—prescriptive versus experiential—used to engage students (Jarvis, 1987a).

Finally, we need to be clear about the type of educative program this study explores. There are, after all, structural and cultural differences between independent adult education divisions at large multiversities and those activities serving adults that are part of broader institutional missions and curricula. A self-contained, adult-oriented school such as the College of Evening and Continuing Education at the University of Cincinnati is an example of the first type. Virtually all community or open-door colleges, by virtue of their inclusion of adult students in the regular flow of academic and cocurricular life, represent the second. In spite of appearances, the former are predisposed to come up short in creating effective adult interventions, while the latter, by refusing to isolate adults in decrepit academic units and therefore fueling campus perceptions of their inferiority, have proven eminently more successful. Hence the exodus of adults to the friendlier confines of the community colleges. The irony here, as before, emerges in the gulf between appearance and reality: one would think that university-affiliated adult programs would have many more resources at their disposal and could easily surpass the academic and cocurricular offerings of local community colleges. As we will see, however, this assumption rests on porous ground which gives way under the slighest pressure.

Further, it must also be conceded that adult education occurs in settings beyond the college campus, a recurring theme in British scholarship (Brookfield, 1983; Jones, 1988; Jarvis, 1992) but often untreated in American research on adult learning. Community centers and corporations have emerged as two of the biggest providers of adult education services. Acknowledging this, however, my investigation will be directed primarily at the adult education colleges and programs existing at larger universities, as it is this venue where past and modern interventions have been best documented. Thus most scholarship has been conducted in or refers to studies in academia, supplying grist for the mill of critical and postmodern reinterpretation.

"Radical," Liberal, and Transformative Adult Education

Throughout these essays, the reader will encounter the term *radical* as a common descriptor. Consequently, use of this term should be made explicit at the outset and therefore eliminate any future ambiguity. In and of itself, there is nothing subversive or revolutionary about the position I take concerning adult education in the ensuing pages. Here the word *radical* is mainly a means of differentiating the nature of this and related writings from the mainstream positions dominating adult education research in the United States (Freiberg, 1979). As long as adult education struggles to define itself and its purposes, adult students will remain relegated to the fringes of academic and campus culture. Therefore, it is imperative for this cohort, already ostracized for traits of Otherness, to participate actively in the debate over how adult programs perceive themselves and what they hope to achieve.

In both this passage and in subsequent sections, the terms *radical, emancipatory,* and *liberatory* are used interchangeably, as is common in critical theory (Ray, 1990). All three describe an educational process having explicit goals of empowerment through increased engagement, consciousness, and action. Tisdell (1993a) articulates the role of liberatory models as striving to deal with and combat systems of hegemony based on gender, race, class, and age. Thus emancipatory education attempts to account for why it is that underserved populations, including adults, are "often silenced or absent" (p. 94) from dialogues on learning and their contributions to the process all too frequently overlooked.

If learning can be comprehended as a vehicle for consciousness raising and ultimately praxis (Freire, 1973)—reflexive action—it also bears resemblance to what is called transformative education (Clark, 1993). Such education is predicated on the idea that students are seriously challenged to assess their value system and worldview and are subsequently changed by the experience. For this to transpire, a renewed sensibility and willingness to act upon critically arrived at knowledge are prerequisites to such transformation. Much of the remainder of this book is about the ways in which we might strive to remake present adult education practice into transformative learning.

At the same time, however, radical education must not be confused with liberal adult education. Historically, liberal education is a legacy of the Enlightenment (Kerr, 1963), a concoction of the modern epoch. It presumes that all people are imbued with a free will, rational mind, essentially moral, and afforded opportunities to pursue individual whim in choosing an academic and life path of their own making. In short, liberal education is anchored in the principle of personal freedom and the luxury to make autonomous choices. Clearly, these ideas would only flourish in a society as naively democratic as the United States, a nation that developed without feudalism and the vestigial class system it bequeathed Western Europe (Fay, 1987). Liberal education, in practice, however, is a far different thing from what philosophers depict. Propositionally, it presumes that both individual will and its "choices are subject to no external restraints" (Paterson, 1979, p. 32), effectively bypassing deep disparities in the economic, social, and political position of diverse groups, all of which mediate against unrestricted exercise of personal choice in yearning to become that to which we truly aspire. In the sense that liberal education seeks to "confirm and emphasize everything we intend to express by education" (p. 38), freeing the rational mind to battle injustice by flexing its new intellectual might for the ennoblement of society, it is a myth.

In assuming that students come to education with a reverence for knowledge as the embodiment of our cultural heritage, liberal education claims to support democracy. In marked contrast, radical education starts with the assumption that people have been socialized differently and are *not* equally empowered to make decisions affecting the course of their lives (Peters, 1980). It is the educator's task to heighten their awareness of the arbitrary and often oppressive relations of power that constitute social reality and pervade its institutions. Only then, at the moment of awakening, can education truly attain its libertarian dreams.

Embracing objectives and anticipating outcomes very distant from the education-for-competency concerns of most programs—a common theme, for instance, in the scholarship of British andragogists (Jones, 1988)—adult educators who recognize and work toward the political fruits of learning earned the sobriquet of a "radical" faction.

SUMMARY

The imputations contained in the phrase "at-risk" are legion. At first glance, the term seems straightforward, implying little more or less than its literal meaning. But there is an insidious side to the "at-risk" iteration. Critical theory informs us that there are multiple inferences replete in language, mostly hidden, some destructive. The power of language in molding educational psychology and opinion must not be underestimated, nor should its colloquializing. The tainting may be subtle, but it is almost always detectable somewhere in popular versions of stories told about disadvantaged groups. For its part, postmodernism warns us that adults, as a new breed of Other, are likely to share the same excluded fate as other marginalized groups whose voices are lost or forgotten in the chorus of the dominant culture.

For many, "at-risk" implies a personal inadequacy rather than a socially engineered one. Consider, as a demonstration, the predilection to speak of "at-risk" students (at any level of schooling) with ambivalence, typically imparting some blame to the individual while assigning a smaller portion to circumstances, as if the precariousness of their place in the school is deserved instead of systemically imposed. "At-risk" students continue to dwell in neighborhoods of academic decay because educators neglect to explore the true source of the problem. Further, the lasting imprint of language (Bannet, 1993), especially disparaging connotations like "at-risk," is too potent for people to question.

It is in the gray area of ambiguity—inadequacy as person-centered or appointed by the institution—that adult students in college find themselves. Do I/they belong? Can I/they succeed? Doubts are harbored across all levels of the institution and in certain circles swells to open incredulity. This negativity does little to foster hope, and perhaps the least persuaded to anticipate success for older learners are professors of the academic creed.

Chapter 3

The Political Economy of Adult Education: A Critical Theory Perspective

> Because higher education is often a prerequisite for disadvantaged groups and a strategic point of access to the mainstream American society, colleges and universities have been focal points in the struggle for personal opportunity and human equality.
> —H. Bowen, *The Costs of Higher Education* (1980)
>
> The *economic* case for higher education begins with the assumption that people and their talents are critical factors of production.
> —A. Carnevale in "Higher Education's Role in the American Economy" (1983)

Critical theory reveals that economic underpinnings support all social formations and thus determine class relations (Leiss, 1972; Hearn, 1973; Zaretsky, 1986). Further, it argues that we cannot truly consider the human condition apart from its capacity to be exploited for production purposes. This "logic of commodification" (Apple, 1989), or extension of capitalistic thinking to academic endeavors, is quite real and in large measure responsible for the anti-egalitarian nature of modern educational practice.

Even noncritical scholars agree that separating economic motives, particularly those endorsed by the state, from educational outcomes may prove difficult. In *Education and Economics* (1971), Rogers and Ruchlin concurred: "The functioning of any mass educational system in the United States is heavily dependent on the policies established to deal with issues of financing, efficiency, and competition" (p. 299) that government authorities espouse.

Focusing on the subject of our immediate concern, former U.S. senior policy analyst at the Department of Health, Education, and Welfare Anthony Carnevale (1983) explored how the interaction of economy, education, and adult students will ultimately affect the future of the country. He noted that higher education institutions have a preeminent economic role in the postindustrial world, but warned that any delay in rising to this task could have disastrous repercussions. "If that national tragedy is to be avoided, the higher education community must articulate and assert its role in the overall performance of the American economy and reapportion some of its services to the needs of an adult clientele" (p. 6).

To this position, critical theory adduces its arguments of how economic concerns affect and often reinforce social relations of dominance and subjugation. In almost all instances, the power of the oppressors and the vulnerability of the oppressed find expression in social institutions—schools and colleges—working to support capitalism.

SCHOOLING AS CLASS REPRODUCTION

Depending on one's location in the political continuum, arguments have been made—benevolent and sinister—on the role schooling plays in social reproduction. Regardless of imputations, this debate is neither recent (Dewey, 1916) nor subsiding (Kerr, 1963). Conservatives like former Secretary of Education William Bennett and his cadre of disciples contend that education is pivotal in the transmission of culture (Smith, 1990) as gleaned from Western, republican, intellectual traditions. Questions of *whose* culture (white, European) it is that is being passed down and the values sustaining it (centrist, capitalist) are rendered subordinate. All we need to know, these conservatives assert, is that educational institutions are predicated on the same democratic, egalitarian principles on which our forbears founded this nation.

Critical theory, concerned with uncovering the dissonances rampant in our social thought, takes a more discriminating view of things. Opposite from the conservative camp, critical educators interpreted the reproduction thesis as a critique of the function that schools and colleges serve in America. Of special concern to them is how these institutions promote class differentiation (Gelpi, 1985) at the primary level of interaction (K-12) and division of labor at postsecondary stages. Henry Giroux articulates this eloquently in *Schooling and the Struggle for Public Life* (1988a, p. 114):

In general terms, schools are reproductive in that they provide different classes and social groups with forms of knowledge, skills, and culture that not only legitimate the dominant culture but also track students into a labor force differentiated by gender, racial and class considerations.

The contrast between defenders of reproduction theory and its attackers is obvious. The former see education as a vehicle of indoctrination into the predominant economic system. Once assimilated, people of every racial, ethnic, and economic class will allow for the rightness of this stratification—as the social institutions such as schools have effectively convinced us for years—and therefore share in its just rewards (Althusser, 1972). In this distorted view, conservatives believe education is the antidote to social inequity. Disparity in material living conditions among differing social classes do indeed exist. However, they are not so acute or without the prospect of being redressed that the poor rebel against what they see only as a temporary disadvantage in the economic order of things. In a fascinating discussion in his *The Culture of Contentment* (1992, p. 10), John Kenneth Galbraith explores how this mass acquiescence came about:

What is new in the so-called capitalist countries—and this is a vital point—is that the controlling contentment and resulting belief is now that of the many, not just the few. It operates under the compelling cover of democracy, albeit a democracy not of all citizens but of those who, in defense of their social and economic advantage, actually go to the polls.

According to Galbraith, the status quo remains unchallenged through the exercise of democracy as reflecting the will not of the majority of people but the *voting* majority, whose grip on power and concomitant social and economic privileges are thus preserved. Inversely, the "underclass" plays its part in the larger economy by supplying the labor to "do the work that the more fortunate do not do and would find manifestly distasteful, even distressing" (p. 33) while clinging to the uniquely American hope that such status is transitory. Thus, by way of consolation, the disadvantaged are placated by something deeply implanted in the American psyche: the conviction that any one of us can, in time and with a little hard work, rise above our circumstances (no matter how cruel) and attain the material comforts. This belief in the undeliverable "promise of classlessness" (Wildavsky, 1991, p. 40) remains fundamental in our cultural mythology.

Higher education advances the interests of the contented majority in securing for them passage into the professions, a better standard of living, and the social prestige bestowed on college graduates. Coming from a different perspective, critical theorists marshal evidence of the hidden, paradoxical messages pervading the entire phenomenon of schooling: the unassailable primacy of Western thought, the imposition of lower academic and ultimately occupational expectations on women and minorities, and consequently the perpetuation of economic divisions through the formal process of education. In aggregate, these effects undermine schooling's libertarian aims.

KNOWLEDGE PRODUCTION AND HUMAN CAPITAL

People are cast in composite: a man, a father, a manager, and a consumer. The common denominator uniting these roles is their impact on micro and macroeconomies (Machlup, 1984). At the lower end, this same man may be the primary income-earner in an extended family of five. At the next layer of production, he may be the owner of a small printing business that employs a dozen workers from the surrounding area. On the macroeconomic level, his business might be one of a thousand minute enterprises affecting the health of the regional economy by generating jobs resulting in production of services and wages that are spent by his employees in purchasing staples for themselves and their families.

This tableau may be seen as a metaphor for education, specifically with universities as academic enterprises. In fact, a prominent economist referred to higher education as the "knowledge industry" (Machlup, 1976). Instead of assembly line goods, however, it manufactures knowledge. The knowledge output coincides with the broader push toward instrumental, utilitarian ends in capitalist cultures. Further, knowledge is given unparalleled value in advanced technological societies. Aronowitz sheds further light on the worth of knowledge: "Society has placed an ideological premium on the acquisition of knowledge for its own sake and an economic premium on the practical, i.e., technical, outcomes of knowledge" (1988, p. 323).

Pure knowledge, then, is sought for its potential returns or derivative academic uses. An example could be a biology professor's gene mapping of the HIV virus which might later serve as the basis for the development of an AIDS vaccine. Because of its innate worth, pure knowledge continues in the university, though the viability of research projects is largely determined now by external influences and funding sources (Fairweather, 1988). (The infringement of commercial interests upon institutional autonomy as two cultures with ostensibly different goals is a fascinating study in itself, but one better left to anthropologists and another time.)

It is applied knowledge, however, that now draws the lion's share of faculty interest and grant-writing time, monopolizes finite institutional R&D resources, and wins the endorsement of university administration since external funding abounds and swifter returns on the investment loom. Increasingly, a laissez-faire atmosphere is gaining a foothold in college laboratories and clinics where immediate economic incentives have taken precedence over the delayed returns tied to pure research.

In this vista, the knowledge production specialists are professors, while the administration manages, markets, and sells the product—educational services—to consumers (Bok, 1982). In turn, these student-consumers bring in their tuition dollars, a steady infusion of capital to sustain the research and development project. The faculty and administration of the academic plant are purveyors of "cultural capital" (Gramsci, 1971), that sum treasure of information, methodologies, codes, and artifacts, an honor accorded them by business, government, and their own parochial traditions. Given the noble charge of both mining and safeguarding knowledge, they thus retain exclusive intellectual property rights and attendant power in the Information Age.

To keep academic industry humming, an unimpeded flow of students (revenue) is necessary. Like any corporation, investment in infrastructure needs to occur for the continued health of the organization. The effort and expense poured into people whose talents support the enterprise is called human capital. Simply put, it denotes the "investment embodied in individuals" (Rogers and Ruchlin, 1971, p. 102). Colloquially, the idea is expressed in the adage that "to make a little you have to spend a little." Obviously, universities commit the greatest share of resources to faculty and administrative overhead as they supply the labor force for this industry. The question theorists might pose, however, would be what proportional investment these same institutions make in their client base, particularly when they are nontraditional.

Perhaps unwittingly, economist Gary Becker provides material for an answer in his *Human Capital* (1975). In a section concerning the relationship between asset appreciation and depreciation (pp. 226–228), he outlines a theoretical reply to the question of why colleges refrain from investing too heavily in the human capital of adult students. Younger students are seen as an outlay for the future. They have years of work, earnings, philanthropy, and social and financial productivity still ahead of them, all of which may be viewed as collateral on the university's investment. At the other end, adult students come to college in the "depreciating" stages of their productive years. Rosen (1975, p. 200) describes this decline in "people's usefulness in the economy" as functional obsolescence. Moreover, adults who completed compulsory schooling (K-12) years earlier acquired knowledge no longer current and who learned skills now outdated are expendable since today's "graduates of high schools and colleges are assumed to be superior to older ones who have suffered obsolescence" (Machlup, 1984, p. 557).

Unfortunately, it appears as though some educators also subscribe to this misconception given their reluctance to subsidize adult education. Proof of their pudding is seemingly offered in the reasons older students typically give for returning to college. They frequently report that their enrollment is the direct result of job displacement, skills deterioration, or functional inadequacy in their chosen vocation (Dillman, Christenson, Salant, and Warner, 1995). Given such self-reports, educational entrepreneurs hesitate to support adult programs.

In contrast, Sheila Slaughter speaks for critical theorists in recoiling from the idea of an "unarticulated comparison between people and physical capital" (1991, pp. 72–73). In an adjacent passage, Slaughter derides the comparison as dehumanizing to students, arguing that the human capital metaphor "likens the education system to the economic system, resting on the premise that education heightens men's and women's abilities to contribute to the production of surplus in the same way capitalist entrepreneurs transform raw materials into profit." She drives home her point in lamenting that using this metaphor aggrandizes the "economic value of higher education above the human."

Aware that American universities are impelled by economic motives and give priority to well-funded graduate education enriched by "foundations, corporations, and government at a rate three times higher than in all of Europe's universities combined" (Simons and Fischer, 1995, p. 46), we begin to understand their disinclination to fund learning programs for older students from whom they expect to reap little financial reward.

KNOWLEDGE, CONTROL, AND THE ADULT STUDENT

Recognizing these conditions, we are brought to the doorstep of a key theme in this chapter: *knowledge is power*. Those dominating the production, dissemination, and transfer of information hold tremendous power in capital-driven society (Carnevale, 1991). With an ever greater emphasis placed on technical and literate workforces, they who hold the keys to graduate and specialized education control access to the professions and exert formidable influence over key sectors—governmental, managerial, and scientific—of the nation's economic climate. This "culture of professionalism" (Bledstein, 1976), or intellectual vanguardism, among academics tends to legitimate their roles as knowledge gatekeepers through exclusionary and undemocratic pretensions to expertise they alone possess (Giroux, 1988a). It is this "guild" mentality—professors as artisans plying a uniquely specialized trade—that compounds the culture of professionalism by encouraging faculty to shift their allegiance from the institution to the confines and cliques of their discipline (Boyer, 1990). As this guild mind-set is patronized by external supporters like corporations and government who enter into such relationships with economic interests, higher education becomes a means of social control by the ruling powers.

The academic plant runs along smoothly when the clients, typically young persons dependent on parental financing and adrift in a sea of messages glamorizing the carnival aspects of university life (recall the film *Animal House*) allow campus officials to mind the store. Though in effect the shareholders, students decline to vote their stock and leave the steering of the university to its own managerial corp (Bowen, 1980), whether or not the course pursued is in the students' actual interest. These tendencies toward disempowering the stockholder and the assertion of bureaucratic dominance were first observed during the 1930s and predicted to be the common future of large economic-minded organizations. This included higher education, which even then was showing signs of closer collaboration with the interests of capital (Berle and Means, 1932). Where things changed, however, was in the influx of adult ex-servicemen following World War II who dramatically differed in their orientation to learning. The preferred clients of the knowledge industry—passive adolescents—gave way to a very different breed in the sophisticated adult student with altogether clearer expectations (Quinnan, 1995a).

Today an adult student presence on campus alters and intensifies customary student-teacher relationships and works to undo the imbalance of power favoring academicians. As faculty authority has remained unimpeachable for centuries (Metzger, 1981), reconstituting the boundaries of student-teacher interaction causes much internal stress. For the first time, professors become agents of resistance against mounting cries for power-sharing and are extremely distressed by it (Riessman, 1980). University culture, long inured to calls for active student involvement in governance, suddenly feels the tremors of change down to its philosophical foundations.

Knowing their tuition payments underwrite the operation of the college, adult learners demand a greater voice in its leadership (Holmes, 1995). Requiring what any discreet investor would, there can be no hidden agendas or secret places in the organization. More than a few academic feathers get ruffled when modifications are proposed, for instance, in the classroom, the product delivery site in the knowledge factory. For its part, the administration often finds itself at odds with older, wiser student-consumers on standard operating procedures designed to keep them at an impersonal distance from decision making (Karol and Ginsburg, 1980), hence the elaborate bureaucratic structures fronting most universities.

The resulting disenchantment between adult students and the academy runs deep. Academics take refuge behind the curtain of academic freedom (Cohen, 1993) whenever any infringement on their production autonomy is detected and dodge a volley of student challenges in this political sanctuary. Administrators respond in the ways they habitually do: creating "ad hoc" committees to deal with leadership issues, then stacking them so heavily with staff and faculty that the few student representatives do not have a fighting chance of introducing change. The culture of the college and its diffused approach to decision making further inhibit innovation:

No individual has much power, not enough to make something happen against moderate resistance. But many have the power to stop an idea or action in its tracks, or at least cause others to pause, deliberate, and compromise to avoid confrontation. Decision-making is difficult at best, even in the most minor matters. (Schaffer, 1992, p. 8)

Suffering from such widespread dysfunction, it is easy to see how a business-as-usual mentality prevails.

Adult learners, quicker to develop an awareness of university methods to quell dissent, are quickly reduced to frustration in trying to reform the power structure along less vertical lines. Rather than continuing the fight against so strong a foe, they relent and resign themselves to "just getting through." To date, I cannot recall an event where adult students, properly agitated, have held protests or conducted demonstrations demanding a broader say in decisions affecting their education. They appear not to have developed the collective consciousness to act en masse for change (Heaney, 1989). It is hoped, however, that encouragement in the form of essays like this and the others in this volume will ameliorate some of their fears and serve as a springboard for action.

THE ETHOS OF INSTITUTIONAL BIAS

It is in this adversarial milieu that adult education programs struggle to exist. Unfortunately, such circumstances do not bode well for the creation of a constructive dialogue. Nor do they imply much in the way of agreement from the university for future commitments of human and material resources for adult education programs. After all, widely divergent perceptions of institutional priorities linger (Hull, 1992, p. 15), and adult interventions usually place comparatively low on the academic totem. However, some consideration of the social perspective on adults in higher education is necessary first.

Exacerbating an already strained relationship are the preconceptions faculty and administrators bring to discussions on how best to serve mature learners. Paradoxically, these notions work to undercut adult student pleas for change, landing on closed ears and minds. Interestingly, this ethos is grounded as much in capitalistic archetypes (Agger, 1989) as it is ingrained in the culture of the organization. For it is widely held, erroneous or not, that in Western societies there is presupposed order to things. Such ordered systems are especially pronounced and inflexible when applied to economic matters. Children play, adolescents attend school, adults labor, and retired persons live off pensions and social security entitlements. Simple and unswerving is our social obedience to this canon. Malcolm Knowles, a luminary in the field of adult learning, speaks to the problem this rationale introduces:

In the prevailing view of society, it is the major task of children to go to school, study and learn, the major task of the adult to get a job and work. In brief, childhood and youth are a time for learning and adulthood a time for working. This is beginning to change, but the dominant thrust of society's expectation and equally of his self- expectation is that for an adult the learning role is not a major element in his repertoire of living. Thus both society and the adult view himself as a non-learner. (1990, p. 157)

Such beliefs comprise the faith of economic determinism, still revered as the hallmark of late capitalism and maintaining a devout following.

Any prolonged opposition to it risks reprisal from the sentries of dominant culture—churches, government, and educational institutions.

Yet there is something more insidious. Residual trust in this doctrine begins to explain the antipathy colleges exhibit in dealing with adult students. In American myth, as retold by Knowles in the previous passage, the concept of adult student is an oxymoron. Adults are providers, heads of households, units of production. If they are in school, they cannot be working. In the unforgiving light of Capital's day, adult students are eschewing their obligation to the free enterprise system. The college, as a preeminent institution dedicated to maintaining social and economic stability (Schon, 1971), implicitly views them as reprobates. The worst sort, this myth tells us, are adults who had jobs, voluntarily gave them up, and have now discovered college as a safe haven in which to rest before returning to productive labor. The inference here being that, to be back in school, adult students must have failed to pass muster in a competitive job market (Gold, 1992). This may be why adult learners enter higher education with attributes comparable to other disadvantaged populations. They, too, are like the Other, deficient in the ways of capitalism and in need of cultural reindoctrination under the auspices of education.

The by-product of such thinking has meant suffering from a culturally transmitted affliction that cripples adult education programs. Faculty, staff, traditional-age students, even adult learners themselves are racked with doubt as to the appropriateness of their assuming a "student" role. Too often they fall prey to the cultural stigma placed on them for playing this part. The staying power of socialization in commerce-driven societies should never be downplayed. Debunking these social myths and companion misconceptions must therefore remain at the forefront of any dialogue on the economy of adult education.

ACADEMIC BUDGETING AS A BATTLEGROUND

The aggregate works (1971, 1979, 1991) of political economist Aaron Wildavsky speak to the sensitive and surreptitious methods of how organizations go about choosing the activities they will support. When applied to academic organizations, a new light is cast upon decision-making processes. As a scholar whose career has been spent studying the politics of resource allocation in social institutions, particularly those avowing egalitarian ends (1991), Wildavsky has produced some very illuminating research. Because universities are highly politicized entities (1979), it stands to reason that the method used to apportion finite resources among competing demands are influenced by power and status. The outcomes of this struggle are publicly recorded in the college budget.

> For our purposes we shall conceive of budgets as attempts to allocate financial resources through political processes. If politics is regarded as conflict over whose preferences are to prevail in the determination of policy, then the budget records the outcomes of this struggle. . . . If organizations are viewed as political coalitions, budgets are mechanisms through which subunits bargain over conflicting goals, make side-payments, and try to motivate one another to accomplish their objectives. (1971, p. 344)

In short, budgeting, like a mirror, reflects institutional priorities as negotiated during a process that could only be characterized as political. Let us fill in some details to comprehend this phenomenon better.

Imagine the university in its factionalized array for a moment. Each college has a specific agenda and interests, its wish list as well as its absolute bottom line, fully aware that to secure a slice of the budgetary pie, negotiations, compromises, and alliances among deans are part of the game. The game is also played at the department level in a relentless scramble for renowned scholars that bring with them bounteous research dollars (Schaffer, 1992). The prestige of having distinguished researchers in the department further enhances the position of that college's dean in bargaining for greater institutional support. In cases where these notables are recognized by broader audiences, which is often the case for law, business, or medical school faculty popularized in local media, the position of the host college in assuring adequate funding is solidified.

Similarly, onus for the success of adult and continuing education colleges in the struggle for funding lies squarely upon the dean or director of the program. It is essential that these leaders understand the political nature of the budgetary process. Where funding decisions are concerned, gentility and unquestioned acceptance of the funding dole must defer to a more urgent consideration—survival. Facing tenuous conditions of financial exigency should resource allocation be anything other than impartial and equitable, adult education deans would be better served to learn Machiavellian methods to secure support than trust in the administration's generosity. Difficult times require less tractable behavior. Too many times adult educators display "resignation about the marginality of their circumstances. They tend not to view their situation as politically created and hence politically alterable, but rather as natural and immutable" (Brookfield, 1986, p. 228). Political skill at the budgeting table is a competency they would do well to acquire.

It is against many Goliaths that adult education programs struggle for support. If indeed academic budgeting is "concerned with the translation of financial resources into human purposes" (Wildavsky, 1979, p. 1), the above scene does not augur well for adult programs. Nonetheless, critical theorists are obliged to ascertain reality behind the facade, and in this instance it has a decidedly political flavor. In sum, academic budgeting involves "managing perceptions, politics, power contests, and personal egos as well as the future of the institution" (Uehling, 1992, p. 8). Since funding determines survivability, the intense competition among differentially empowered academic players in the budgeting process stands as an unabating source of anxiety for educators of adults. If adult programs depend on the largesse of the university but are presumed to be deficient in the quality of their academic and student programs as well as their contribution to the economic well-being of the institution, this information must be seriously weighed by educators for what it implies.

ORGANIZATIONAL RESPONSE

Stated plainly, the plethora of academic services provided to adult learners are illusory. Like mirages shimmering on the desert floor, these programs lure us with ethereal beauty from a distance. The closer we draw, however, the thinner they become until the allure dissipates into barely visible structures and services. If this language is too flowery, others prefer rhetoric that is coldly realistic. Holmes (1995) begs her readership to stop "thinking of adult education as a 'stepchld' of the educational system and adult educators as 'moonlighters' " (p. 14), a far too frequent inclination in her observations in the field.

Yet there are reasons for these aspersions. An eminent educator has observed: "Higher education, like all other forms of production, is subject to diminishing returns. . . . As higher education expands, it may attract less qualified . . . students, which may also bring about reductions in incremental outcomes" (Bowen, 1980, p. 12). In this, Bowen is stating that a negative correlation exists between increased enrollments that relax admissions standards and a market glut of mediocre college graduates. In the law of supply and demand, this translates into a saturated market and decreases the value of the product being vended. Thus, by accepting and educating anything other than the "ideal" student—and we can guess who that is *not*, academic institutions endanger the prominent role entrusted to them in shaping the larger economy.

In the remaining discussion, I draw upon my own career experiences from the College of Lifelong Learning (CLL) at Wayne State University, an urban multiversity in Detroit. Though I dare not declare them to be representative across the field of adult education, I believe they contain lessons worth sharing and invite the reader to judge their ultimate value.

Much of the time, adult learning programs are ephemeral, always within sight but never quite tangible. Deans are appointed, courses scheduled, and faculty recruited to teach. But the theoretical and moral scaffolding supporting these interventions waver from the lack of solid foundation. Falling back on budget formulae that claim economy of scale, institutions endow departments along prestige and income-producing criteria (Fairweather, 1991). This being so, the pattern of resource allocation may be construed as reflection of institutional priorities. In this reality, any hope for equity is removed from the distribution of funds in perhaps the oldest lesson of power politics: the haves get more, while the have-nots receive even less. This script was sadly reenacted in the troubled financial saga of the College of Lifelong Learning.

As a strong, independent teaching and research faculty within the College of Lifelong Learning did not exist to champion its cause or demonstrate its scholarly mettle before the full university, adult programs sponsored under the auspices of the College invariably settled for scraps from the budgetary table. Compounding this already dismal situation was the fact that CLL's dean operated largely outside the council of deans. For personal reasons never made clear, he preferred the maverick role to that of ally or partner. Being the rogue, however, he further isolated a college already teetering on the brink of a financial precipice by failing to negotiate budgetary arrangements with better positioned deans. Ironically, it was such an alliance that might have improved CLL's status in the university rather than reinforcing its role as a pariah.

Its short supply of shielded resources made it especially vulnerable to retrenchment during bad times and predatory attack from established "fiefdoms" (Boyer, 1990) during good in the endless tussle for recognition against politically stronger opponents within the university.

The outlook was bleak. Understaffing and underfunding hurt but did not kill. A funding system characterized as laissez-faire, or economic survival of the fittest, however, could. At CLL, where many of its programs relied on "soft money" (self-generated from Continuing Education Units (CEU) offerings rather than subsidized by the university), it nearly did.

Interestingly, the survival of revenue-draining fine arts schools in public and private universities indicates how skilled academic politicians can mask their agendas. They offer music and drama courses as evidence of fair play in diverting monies from a limited pool to support the university's aesthetic aims. What they choose not to disclose is the patronage these activities cultivate in the larger community. The bequeathing of sizable estates by cultural impresarios in the community to arts-friendly colleges in recent years—and there have been many—stand as ready testimony.

Sadly for its students, adult education promises little such prospect of windfall for the university. This is acutely true for baccalaureate or certificate-level programs. Since adults who enroll in them are viewed as displaced and financially marginal to begin with, the chance that at some point in the future they will return to endow the college is dubious. Prejudicially speaking, these individuals have affirmed their stature as outcasts in the production process, or else they would be meaningfully employed. Knowing this, the knowledge industry begs off investing too heavily in opportunities for adult learning.

As a final effort at validation, I offer the evening, weekend, and sprint courses of study for the professions at the College of Lifelong Learning as portraits in contradiction. These programs were undergraduate level, among them were nursing (L.P.N) and teacher certification programs. They were, by any estimation, no more poorly articulated than those found at the next university. Yet because of the problems already mentioned—erroneous preconceptions, uncommitted faculty, apolitical administrators, and financial problems—they remained academically suspect. Of course, dramatically different circumstances surrounded the graduate degree programs catering to working or "professional" adults. These were usually packaged by rival colleges within the university as the "Executive MBA" or "Part-Time Juris Doctor," removing CLL from the playing field. Handsome publications were constructed, targeted radio and television spots produced, and staff specially groomed in treating executive-trainees were selected and installed in lavish college offices. Since students gravitating toward such programs were already professional people with solid footholds in corporate

America, they experienced far fewer of the organizational and cultural barriers their economically disadvantaged counterparts did in undergraduate adult education. However this phenomenon is viewed, it uncovers inconsistencies in the way colleges attend to various sets of adult students. Those who have established professional credentials and are pursuing more specialized degrees employable in the service of capitalism receive a remarkably different greeting than adults struggling to obtain a liberal education.

THE ILLUSION OF OPPORTUNITY

Ideally, any new understanding of the political economy of the adult condition in colleges and universities should result in proactive institutional response, if not for the sake of these students, then at least to lend an appearance of judicious concern and thoughtful reaction (Shriberg, 1980).

Once again, however, the academy is stricken by polarization, and adult education becomes the first casualty. Society has imposed two opposing agendas upon higher education and expects both, regardless of the gulf between them, to be met (Parnell, 1990). This conflict is the endless debate over access versus quality. Economists call this the problem of diminishing returns: as a specialized trade or service is opened to more and more trainees—in this case higher education to larger numbers of students—its worth in the marketplace declines (Simmons, 1995). When considered in its economic context, this dilemma threatens to inflame even the most placid discussion among educators into an intellectual brawl. As is often the case, critical theory shows us that much of the vitriol swirling around the debate stems from the language used in the discussion. Since language, like all forms of social expression, is infused with ideological connotation not necessarily familiar to minority individuals, conflicts arise. Parnell (1990, pp. 160–161) stresses the point that access and quality, *in themselves*, are neither mutually exclusive nor mutually supportive concepts. Rather, it is through our own cognitive filter (in this instance, bias) that we choose to impart an adversarial or reconcilable inference. Both notions have implications concerning the economy, and therefore the power, of education; therefore, faculty, taking sides according to personal prejudices, make the debate extremely volatile.

How can higher education succeed in producing a body of highly capable engineers, researchers, and managers if its ranks are diluted by seriously undertalented segments of the population simply to placate the demands of the egalitarians? In an ever shrinking world and global commerce, can the United States retain a competitive edge if the products of its educational factories are anything less than the best and the brightest? Crusaders for quality first believe that the fortunes of our nation are being risked by those who would opt for social opportunity over economic might (Carnevale, 1991). Adult students, belittled by academic purists as the new recipients of entitlements formerly spent on other disadvantaged groups, are hastening the decline of our competitive position by usurping resources better spent upon more deserving student cohorts. The battle between these agendas continues to rage in institutions and appears no nearer resolution than it was twenty years ago when adults began coming to college in sizeable numbers (Cross, 1971).

If the academy persists in doubting the economic necessity of sponsoring adult education, those students enrolled in these programs feel equally certain of their place. Like their younger colleagues, mature learners cling to the popular notion of education as the surest ticket to social mobility. Concomitantly, this mobility promised an economic edge as well. It is another aphorism in the pantheon of American culture, one that began in the aftermath of World War II (Quinnan, 1995a) and continued through subsequent generations.

Yet once again there remains an inconsistency, an ugly truth to militate against the belief in education's capacity to overcome disadvantage. Michael Apple (1989, p. 137) touches on this paradoxical element in declaring:

As we have just seen, for many of the American people, even when educational levels and "skills" are equalized, the economy has *not* been as responsive as the theory behind the reports would have it. Education is not the solution to the bulk of these problems. Existing and quite widespread conditions of discrimination, exploitation, and inequality—that is, structural conditions generated by the economy . . . and by governmental policies that largely reproduce these conditions—are among the root causes.

The case Apple makes complements the position of critical theory in isolating the rift between "what is and ought to be" (Horkheimer, 1974)—or illusion and reality. On the surface, it is widely supposed that a college education enhances one's chances for better career opportunities and a materially higher standard of living. Regrettably, the reality of modern existence is that countless forms of discrimination thrive in the present world and adversely impact the lives of many people.

Aware of these repressive circumstances, it is no wonder that Americans, especially those living on the economic margins, find hope for redemption in education. For adult students who count on experience as referents on the map of life, learning is the last recourse to economic and social parity in an otherwise indifferent environment.

ADULT EDUCATION AS CAREER TRAINING

Although it is self-evident that adults come to college for the purpose of updating technical and transferrable skills that will make them more marketable in the job market, this cannot be assumed as a foregone conclusion. If there is even a smattering of other factors motivating adults to attend college, why do universities insist on developing adult education programs that stress only career (Cervero, 1988) rather than intellectual or emotional benefits? Further, why do educators and theorists suffer from a mental occlusion allowing them to envision adult learning only as preprofessional training instead of something that stimulates personal and cognitive growth (Chickering and Havighurst, 1981)?

Scores of studies begin with the premise of education for career advancement where mature persons are concerned. In fact, this author had a difficult time locating any research pertinent to the adult education that *did not* succumb to overused arguments for skills development, literacy training, or technical preparation as primary themes. John Naisbett and Patricia Aburdene's *Megatrends 2000* (1990) is a good example in exhorting this link between education and occupation: "Finally, the 120 million people in the U.S. work force today must constantly upgrade their skills over the course of the 1990's. It will require a tremendous human resource effort to transform corporate America into the decentralized, customer oriented model of the information society" (p. 127). Indeed, the sheer scale of this image is hard to resist, perhaps illustrating why most scholarship looking at the adult education-economy correlation predominates in the research.

Undoubtedly, many adults do indeed participate in learning to improve a job situation and ultimately their upward mobility (Dillman, Christenson, Salant, and Warner, 1995). As a majority are self-supporting or heads of families, this makes perfect sense. As we have seen, most Americans look at college as an investment in their future. A large part of this future depends on standard of living and economic security. On my own campus, an open-access branch of a major university, our community relations division recently debuted a program for mature students driven by the unabashed slogan "Learn More, Earn More." Predictably, early indications show that this campaign promises to be our most successful in making inroads into the local adult community. Perhaps more credence should be given to those declaring the indissoluble link between education and jobs. Conservative economist Anthony Carnevale confidently articulates this view in claiming that the "new social compact" is one based on work. "A job is the price of admission to this individualistic culture and participatory polity. People unable to find work eventually disappear from the community, drop out of the political system, and fall into the underground economy" (1991, p. 88). This fatalistic appeal to our all-too-human dread of failing, of anonymity, of oblivion, is too strong for most to ignore. Such is the political economy of postmodern America.

Adult education, then, must be concerned with occupational issues to a certain extent. The critical error lies in thinking that career considerations should be the beginning and end of planning services for adults. Mounty (1991, p. 43) does a magificent job of representing this position in stating that adult "students expect college to 'teach' them how to get a job after graduation." I and others struggle with the idea that profit incentives are so omnipresent that we deny the prospect of any personal motives—as Knowles spent a life documenting—to learn. Obliged to expose the inconsistencies between intent and reality, we once again return to critical theory for direction. This theory informs us that mechanistic views of education—for example, reproducing the systems and structures of capitalism—are incomplete. Just as they occur in discussions about younger students, educators must expand the scope of their dialogues to include issues of self-concept, critical thinking, economic empowerment, and cultural awareness. Too often, debate over how to address the needs of adults are bereft of these crucial issues.

POST-INDUSTRIALISM AND THE INFORMATION AGE

Sometime in 1955—the precise date is inexact—the Information Age succeeded the Industrial Era. This was the first year since such statistics were kept that more people worked in service, communications, and data-related jobs than in manufacturing (Matthews and Noorgard, 1984). Although 1955 passed quietly, and apart from a handful of government economists no one paid much attention, the implications for society were monumental. For in the postmodern age, knowledge would emerge as the single most important commodity a firm or individual could possess.

The migration of Americans to cities was a second silent but no less immense social phenomenon (Elliott, 1994) announcing the advent of the postmodern economy. In 1920, the population was almost evenly distributed between rural and urban areas, 48.8% to 51.2% respectively (U.S. Department of Commerce, 1990). By 1990, U.S. Census data reveals that 75.2% of the American population resided in urban areas. Impetus for the exodus is not hard to deduce: when the jobs went to the cities, the people followed. In that same period, higher education began expanding to urban areas from the small towns and cloistered hamlets of the ivory tower.

For academic institutions, the consequences of this mass movement were just as far-reaching. In addition to broadening access and diversifying enrollments, there were also significant economic factors:

Urbanization, a different economic base, and quantum leaps in technology as well as longer life spans and intense global competition are all changes in society that have major implications for higher education in the United States. When millions of industrial jobs vanish and are replaced by jobs in service and knowledge-based industries, the need and demand for access to higher education increases. (Elliott, 1994, p. 6)

More than other segments, adults felt most directly the impact of this shift in the economic base. The elderly were retired, and the young, still in school, could be properly prepared. But where did that leave adults as the generation caught in the middle of this economic revolution? Recognizing that an updating of skills and knowledge were essential for survival in the global village, they returned to higher education. What they often found was an institution indifferent, even hostile, to their circumstances.

In many ways, college remains the territory of the young and inexperienced. Mature persons, society intimates, should not be here but gainfully employed instead. Long-standing social and academic expectations cast adult learners in the role of resident alien. They may enroll, but not as a fully respected or empowered force in the learning community. Oversimplified prescriptions misinformed us that teaching and cocurricular systems devised for adolescent minds really only needed to be tweaked for the "new student" (Cross, 1981) rather than razed and rebuilt. Eventually, their cries were heard, programs were created, and trustingly adults came. But they entered with the hope of equal opportunity and autonomous participation. Critical theory suggests that their purity of intention was misplaced. The gap between the service they expect and the education they actually receive is genuine and distressing.

Resistance to their presence stems primarily from the economic reasons examined earlier. In capitalist societies, discrimination, when stripped of its physical characteristics (color, age, sex), is engendered by a perceived threat to the economic hierarchy. Buttressing this hierarchy are corporations, government, and universities. Together they determine national economic policy, domestic spending priorities, and those who will prosper as well as those who will not. Too often adult students find themselves among the latter group on the economic margins.

Chapter 4

Adult Students' "Stories of Struggle": A Critical Field Study

Where critical theory, especially the educational genus, has long been susceptible to attack is in its lack of field trial and application to actual learning settings (Ellsworth, 1989). In abstraction, as philosophy, during conceptual debate, it performs admirably as a forceful method of inquiry. But how well does it hold up under empirical conditions? If it proves useful only in the bookish precincts of the academy (Heller, 1995) but buckles under testing in the field, then critical and postmodern theories fall dreadfully short in living up to their emancipatory claims.

In a limited-run university publication titled *Closing the Doors: Stories of Struggle at U.C.*, University of Cincinnati English professor Martha Stephens assembled a narrative collage of the "economic ordeals" (1993, p. 1) faced by today's students and their families. As it was published before I came to that university, I first learned of it through an article in the *Utne Reader*, a forum of the alternative press, which heralded it as a call to arms in the student war on class bias. Two years later, after taking a position at this same institution, I contacted Dr. Stephens to obtain a copy of this by now hard-to-come-by document. After a few weeks of silence, I arrived at my office one day to find two copies of the text along with a pleasant note from the author wishing me well in my own research.

Stories of Struggle arose out of a running assignment Dr. Stephens gave to students enrolled in her second-year Topics in Literature course. The theme of the course was literature and society and included a wide sampling of political readings from Thomas Paine through Karl Marx as well as other notable thinkers who set forth ideas about economic and social struggle. In brief, the students were asked to write "reaction papers" to the readings and class discussion by borrowing from their own experiences in financing a college education. The booklet included full and partial passages from thirty-three essays.

Although Stephens' probable motivation in giving the assignment may have been the "social conscience" she acknowledged is a compelling part of her personality, she does not describe herself as a radical educator or *Stories* as social activism. Her intentions, simply, were to collect individualized accounts of the economic barriers students confront in attending a large urban university. The transcendental quality in her work is relived through those instances where students face down these impediments, often overcoming them, yet just as many times faltering at a painful psychological cost.

In the main, the assignment evoked replies that primarily addressed financial anxieties. Social and cultural nuances appear and at times tantalize but usually remain underdeveloped afterthoughts to the student's immediate concern over meeting the requirements of the assignment. To truly touch the emotion present in them, considerable time exploring their implications would be necessary.

If Stephens was satisfied merely to chronicle, I pondered long over how forcefully critical and postmodern interpretations could extract, layer by layer, the personal hope and sorrow woven into these tales. My idea seemed confirmed by the author's own observation that the students' papers "poured out somewhat like small oral histories might be poured out, but perhaps not to be valued for less than that" (Stephens, 1993, p. 3).

To a scholar excited by transformative educational initiatives, the soul in these tellings provide priceless material for critical analysis. In each student's tale, elements of hardship and glimpses of alienation emerge. Against the privileged backdrop of academia in its traditional form, their struggles supply stark contrast in speaking to the darker realities of university life for many students who simply view themselves as ordinary.

Finally, the one sustained and perhaps valid attack on critical scholarship is its aversion to field trial in depicting the oppressive conditions marginalized student cohorts encounter. Since recollections were printed in the students' own voices, from their own memories, in their vernacular, a richer lode of raw material ready for conceptual refinement could rarely be found. Below appears one such account from *Stories of Struggle*.

AMY'S STORY

A moving tale emerges in the story of Amy, an unmarried mother on state-assisted living, and the trying circumstances she endured to complete her education.

Twenty months ago, my life changed dramatically. I became pregnant. I was living on my own, in Virginia, working a minimum wage job. I had no car and no medical insurance because I had just recently begun working at my job. I had to travel over a mountain to get to the hospital where medical cards for hardship cases were taken. I was in quite a mess. . . .

I was devastated. I gathered up the few belongings I had, a bed I had recently purchased and a TV given to me by a friend, and headed back home to my parents' home in Ohio.

After months of wondering whether or not to place the child for adoption, I decided to "join the growing number of single mothers," as I've heard others put it. It was not an easy decision to say the least. I was amazed at the expenses I would have. They were so different from when I lived on my own.

School is my job now. I must work now at getting a good education so that I won't live on the edge of poverty for the rest of my life.

I'm not used to working an outside job. (Motherhood and full-time school are definitely jobs!) I had my first job, at a donut shop, two weeks after I turned sixteen. I often held more than one job. . . .

Now it costs me to have work. I tried to find a job, but I just couldn't make enough money. Day-care costs at least sixty dollars a week, if you can find someone to take your child into their home. Day-care centers average from sixty to seventy-five dollars a week, not counting disposable diapers, if they have any openings in your child's age range.

I am often embarrassed by my position. People treat you differently when you're on welfare or "public assistance," as I like to call it. I think a lot of people in this class would look at me differently if they knew I was an unwed welfare mother. I've seen it happen too many times not to notice the reaction. I understand prejudice but am fortunate enough to be able to hide my "unsavory" characteristic. . . .

I am fortunate, I suppose, that my education is being paid for by the government. There are tremendous problems in this payment though. Each dollar must be accounted for. Each dollar not assigned for a specific purpose costs me a dollar. Plus, I get very negative treatment from financial aid officers when they find out my situation (unless this is my own ultrasensitivity).

I've grown a lot since March of 1988. Probably more than I should have. Definitely more than I wanted to. Don't get me wrong—I'm happy. I have a wonderful, healthy, happy, bright little boy named Philip Alexander. I'm just at a place where I never, in my wildest dreams expected to be. School is my way out. I've got to go to every class—for my son, for myself, and for our future. (p. 25)

Analysis

Amy's account begins with some background on the nature of both the economic and social realities sharply defining her life. The observation that she had no medical insurance is as frightening to her as the fact that she was stuck in a low-paying, menial job and unable to find transportation across miles of rough country. Despite the aggregate wealth of the United States, most of its citizens, like Amy, are mortally terrified at the prospect of being stricken with an illness that requires extended health care, aware that the costs associated with ongoing treatment translate into ruin. Feeling unwanted social pressure from being an unwed mother, Amy opted to keep the child after anguishing over a decision that many lower-income but few affluent women are forced to make every day. Choice, despite the claims of both sides in the abortion debate, seems to be a luxury the disadvantaged do not enjoy equally. The decision to return to college was made, but very nearly at the price of a child she almost never knew.

Another facet of her story that further bespeaks her dilemma concerns the shame Amy expresses when people learn of her circumstances. Particularly horrifying to her is the prospect that classmates, most of whom are late adolescents relying on parents for financial support, will discover her terrible secrets—a fatherless infant and subsisting on welfare, two things certain to identify her as "different" from traditional-age peers. Amy's psychology is also revealing in the duality it displays. On the one hand, we get an inkling that she is personally proud of her decision to have and keep the child on her own. Amy recognizes that hers was a difficult dilemma and one taking moral courage to resolve. On the other hand, however, are the fears she holds regarding society's view of her as "unsavory." Where her resolve weakens is in contemplating the social stigma attached to being a welfare mother and the shame it would bring upon her in being discovered by others.

But Amy, like all adults, has lived long enough to feel the sting of cultural mores and experience the hardship of economic inequality. Much of what comes through in her writings are regretful ruminations on these experiences as they predict how others will likely assess her situation. One such bittersweet moment surfaces in her recounting, but not articulating, the humiliation of having to account for every dollar the government provided by way of support. Although she expresses chagrin at being forced to do so, Amy accepts this onerous duty with resignation since, after all, she is surviving on the bounty of the state.

It is clear in her tale, however, that she hopes would-be critics, fellow students and teachers premier among them, will acknowledge that she has grown and become more responsible through her struggle. Although the path immediately ahead is rocky, she continues to work toward self-reliance. Further, like all Americans, Amy tenaciously clings to a conviction that school will ultimately prove her social salvation, her "way out," affording career and life opportunities that usually pass over women in similar circumstances.

STORIES OF STRUGGLE—A NEW LOOK

Amy's story was one of the few tellings from an adult student in the original *Stories* pool. However, since our emphasis here is on adult learners, wider use of Stephens' material would lead us away from our chosen subject. Still, her work germinated the idea for a similar piece of investigation, only with an audience comprised entirely of adult students.

The research framework for this study is the larger work in which this chapter is situated. Problem statement, review of the literature, and research methods have already been amply detailed in other chapters. They provide both the theoretical and empirical context for this investigation. Further, the analyses that follow are informed by critical and postmodern theories and their insistence on giving voice to the oppressed. Discussion of the data presented in this chapter would be less forceful under any other interpretive mode, for it is their emphasis on class injustice and cultural bias that enliven the collected accounts.

Deaning in a two-year, branch college of the University of Cincinnati, I had a natural pool of nontraditional adult learners to draw upon. Here at Raymond Walters College, the median student age is 29. Related demographic data of importance show that 68% of the enrollment is female, while 62% of the total enrollment is part-time, indicating they divide their day between school, work, and domestic responsibilities. This nontraditional profile also suggested that a rich vein of stories might be mined for the study.

An open-ended survey was developed by the author to solicit from students their impressions of what life as an adult learner had meant to them. A hypothesis was that, in the narrative replies, students would unconsciously identify visible or perceived barriers putting their educational plans "at-risk." The following questions were posed:

1. Please share your experiences as an *adult* student, positive and negative, in dealing with faculty, staff, and other students. Include experiences from inside and outside the classroom
2. Do you think being an adult student has resulted in an educational experience similar to or different from other students?
3. If different, how?

Approximately 26 surveys were returned from students enrolled in a Sociology of the Family course offered in the Fall quarter of 1995. Preconsultation with the instructor indicated that, with rare exception the majority of participants in the class would in fact be adults. A check of the responses indicated that 25 of 26 were indeed filed by students 22 years of age or older. In fact, the age range of respondents ran from 20 to 49.

Names of survey participants do not appear in subsequent discussion, as they were guaranteed anonymity. The only three bits of personal data I requested were demographic: age, race/ethnicity, and sex. Therefore, all excerpts and quotations are attributed to "respondents" or "survey participants" instead of properly named or fictional individuals.

SOURCES OF STRUGGLE

Abundant material came from the collected replies, which, through the process of refining, promised to serve as a teeming source of information upon which several assumptions of critical and postmodern theory might be tested. Issues of power, class, and diversity were likely to be raised.

Participant responses were grouped into several thematic categories revolving around self-reported problems and concerns. The taxonomy that evolved might best be seen as reflecting those sources of struggle that adults confront in academic environments. At least two respondents had to mention an item for a category to be created. As a result, it was possible to assemble the data into six categories:

Response Clusters

1. Economic barriers
2. Internal family stressors
3. Student-to-student tensions
4. Student-teacher strains
5. Organizational obstacles

Interestingly, there was an unanticipated evenness in the distribution of comments across these clusters, which surprised the researcher. Preliminary expectations held that the first response set, economic barriers, would garner the most commentary. The sole exception to this pattern surfaced in the category detailing student-to-student tensions. Here is the distribution curve:

Response cluster:	1	2	3	4	5
Number of Comments:	8	7	12	7	7

Supplied with a wealth of qualitative data, I then set about examining the information contained in each response set, including quotations taken from actual student accounts and interpreting both themes and patterns using the conceptual frameworks generated by critical theory and postmodernism.

1. Economic Barriers

Critical theory asserts that the economically disadvantaged suffer disproportionately in capitalist societies (Dickinson and Russell, 1986; Marcuse, 1989a). Unfortunately, they also shoulder the added burden of social indifference in attempting to rise above dire circumstances and make use of the public opportunities—education—that could improve their status. Adult students, frequently enrolled in college to offset a career or personal crisis having negative economic effects, may be regarded as so disadvantaged.

Not unexpectedly, a large number of respondents identified financial difficulties as an integral, if not central, part of their struggle to attend college. One student said it most succinctly:

Since I work full-time, my course load is limited (6 credits), but I have many other responsibilities besides homework and my job. My husband is also a student (part-time now), and due to limitations in financial aid, of which we were totally unaware, he is also working to pay for his education.

Compounding their difficulties, federal and state financial aid programs usually offer little to augment the finite resources older learners have at their disposal.

I have had to finance my education through school loans. There was no way for us to save enough money for me to go back to school, and being as we are an average, working, middle-class family and own a modest home, I was not eligible for any grants.

Because the respondents are adults, they are self-supporting and must assume the cost of tuition in addition to other financial obligations such as mortgage payments or rent, food, transportation, and child care. "School is the hardest obstacle to overcome," one respondent admitted; "because of work I can't *just* go to school. I *have* to work to pay for college, and my apartment, and my car, and my bills."

Unlike their teenage classmates, they are not living off the generosity of parents or relatives, though family members often lend a helping hand in terms of part-time or occasional day care. But even this assistance they make use of reluctantly. This student expressed regret, mixed with shame, at putting family members through leaner times for her decision to enroll: "It also makes it difficult having only one income. Because I go to school full-time, I do not work. Therefore, the burden of bringing in money lies solely on my husband."

Adult learners are not oblivious to the fact that this combination of responsibilities—work, family, studying—minimizes the prospect of experiencing other aspects of campus life. As a 26-year-old student observed: "Now that I'm on my own and working two jobs to stay afloat, my social life has become a thing of the past," further lamenting the idle hours younger students have to enjoy the total experience but often squander away "partying."

Financial independence and self-sufficiency are common traits among adult students and ones of which they are fiercely proud. Many have gone to great lengths to make education affordable and achievable. "One of the hardest obstacles I have had to face is finances and paying for my education. I joined the Army as a means to pay for my education. Otherwise, I would not be here."

In spite of competing priorities, adult students shift monies they could be using for other important items to education. This indicates a willingness to forgo the material comforts, even to incur personal and family hardships in order to pursue educational objectives. Consider what one student said in this regard:

It is hard to come up with the cash to pay for my classes . . . And we can't afford for me to quit work and go to school full time. If I quit work we wouldn't have enough money to have hardly anything, much less for school. With my income now it goes to pay for classes and books. But it is well worth it.

Dreams invariably sustain them, and even in the most spartan circumstances this adult student remained dedicated to her academic plans.

2. Internal Family Stressors

Because the work ethic of a Puritan past is so sacred in American lore, friction often arises within the family of an adult student when the spouse or children feel the adult student is refusing to follow the path our culture dictates and instead opts for what some regard as the leisure activity of education (Wilson, 1981). The gender card, where it exists, also comes into play. Many adult students are women (in this survey, 23 of 26 respondents). As we have seen, society has fairly rigid perceptions about roles appropriate for women (Tisdell, 1993a)—mother, spouse, single parent—and these expectations crystallize as the life cycle progresses. When a wife or mother chooses to become a student, she is certain to experience this role-shifting. One student declared: "Being a female, I have to juggle a full-time job, 3 children, a grandchild, husband, and a large extended family with my education." Another individual proudly noted, "Since the summer of 1988, I have only missed *one day* of class. (My son was born that day). I was back in school for my next class, five days later." Emotionally fragmenting as constantly changing roles could be, many respondents exhibited a stubborn pride in their capacity for adaptation.

For some adults, concerns about stress put on their marriage were paramount. A student commented about the tension attending college caused between herself and her husband:

Going back to school has sometimes been hard on my marriage also. My husband sometimes thinks I pay more attention to my homework than to him. He is probably right though. I do pay an awful lot of attention to my school work.

Another respondent approached the same concern from a slightly different angle:

With my husband and myself in school, it was hard at first to make time for "fun" since we were both involved in full-time jobs (and school). But we both agreed that the education we were getting was very important and we've learned to work around our schedules to find time that is just for us.

Other survey participants expressed regret over the fact that domestic obligations prevented them from wider involvement in campus

activities. A representative comment emerges in the following statement:

First of all, being a female and a mother, my priorities are taking care of my
family and making sure that they eat well and are safe. Therefore I do not have
extra time to participate in any kind of extracurricular programs. . . . I feel like
being married is an obstacle to interaction with younger students.

In a few instances, adult students spoke to the criticism they endured
from parents and friends about their involvement in learning and
complaints about divided loyalties. A 39-year-old student ruminated:

The strain on family life is harder as an adult student. It has been hard for me
to juggle going to school part-time, spend time with my 3 children (ages
11–18) and my husband, and then work every weekend. The one good thing
is that they have gotten more independent and my husband has had to accept
more responsibility for child care and family life, which he needed to do.

Family members can also impart a measure of guilt in reminding adult
students of the social pressures against education for any but the young.
Accusing them of distorted priorities was a typical tactic, according to those
surveyed. Responding to the guilt these others brought to bear, one adult
conceded that "I feel there is a constant struggle to divide my time and
energy evenly" between the academic and personal dimensions of her life.

3. Adult Student-Younger Student Tensions

As college is usually considered the province of the young and strong
social norms reinforce this belief, adult students are not always wel-
comed by younger colleagues. Sensing the antipathy directed toward
them in addition to coping with self- generated doubts about academic
ability (Chism, Cano, and Pruitt, 1989), adults often spoke unflatter-
ingly of youthful classmates. Sentiments such as "I am more mature
and more dedicated than younger students" or "we (adults) have much
more at stake than younger students who don't know what they want
out of life and don't pay for their own education" echoed repeatedly
throughout the gathered responses.

If older students agree that a peculiar tension sometimes develops in
relations with these peers, the cause of it does not surprise them. More
often than not, adults mention the carefree and careless lives traditional
students lead and how this contributes to the immature attitude they
display toward their studies.

I see students who are just coming in out of high school who have no responsibilities other than school work. They have parents to pay for their education, cook their meals, shop for them, pay the bills, etc. In my family, *I* am the one who does these jobs plus study.

Another mature learner, age 24, observed: "I sit in class sometimes with students who are here right from high school and know how different it is for me than for them. They seem not to care as much as I do." In a later passage, this same respondent speculates that differences in psychological and life stages account for the disparity. If one is familar with the work of developmental psychologists from Piaget to Erickson, as well as adult educators from Knowles to Cross, this respondent's conjecture was very near the mark.

Additionally, adult students often decried what they perceive as a lack of responsibility symptomatic of a wider indifference affecting younger peers. Many respondents mentioned hearing adolescent students talking about partying, "road trips," or football games, while at the same time planning to cut classes and delay completing assignments to tend to these social events. One reported:

Last night in my class, three 18-year-olds were talking about skipping class next week to go to a rock concert. I think that adult students realize the importance of a degree and would not consider skipping for something so minor.

This 34-year-old student and mother of three was less restrained in her criticisms:

I overheard two girls (18–19, I think) talking in the elevator. "God, I hate when it rains. I hate coming to school when it rains—it's so depressing. . . . If it's like this tomorrow, I'm not coming to class." The mother in me wanted to scream, "your parents aren't paying for you to go to school only when it's convenient in your schedule, missy."

Another respondent was more wistful, opining that "With age comes wisdom, confidence and self-reliance. On the other hand, age also brings the realization that life is not all fun and games."

To older learners, traditional-age students appear demonstrably less serious about their studies, come to class unprepared, and contribute little to class discussions. For its part, the research (Jacobs, 1989; Lynch and Bishop-Clark, 1994) shows that younger students frequently see adults as monopolizing class and instructor time, are combative about philosophical points in class discussions, and are preoccupied with recounting life experiences as learning examples.

The uneasiness a few respondents detected in their relationships with younger learners manifested itself in still other forms. One adult student, 49 years old, claims that her physical presence and transference issues might be factors compounding misconceptions each group holds about the other. "Many younger students have not resolved issues with their own parents and are suspicious of interaction with me. (I'm very maternal in appearance.)" A different individual remembered the impression she was left with after a recent dealing with younger counterparts: "If you stop and ask a question of a fellow student (especially the very young ones) sometimes you are looked at like 'you have to be crazy—you should know that at your age.' "

"Although at times I have an advantage because I can bring years of life experience and accumulated knowledge to a class," waxed one adult student, "I find the class situation can still be difficult if people (young and older) weren't here to learn." Adults, cognizant of the experiential bond they share, indicate a preference for learning activities where other adults participate. A Hispanic female, age 33, underscored the importance of learning in the company of age-mates as they bond into an enclave of Otherness in the midst of unfamiliar territory: "I feel very comfortable at this College with so many students my age and older. It keeps me from feeling out of place."

One way of coping with the estrangement that seems to exist between older and age-differentiated students and threatens to interfere with the learning process has been suggested. According to two researchers, it is incumbent upon the instructor to create a climate of mutual respect and trust. This can be achieved by acknowledging and candidly discussing issues of age(ism) with the class participants in an attempt to lower "resistances to working with differently aged students" (Lynch and Bishop-Clark, 1994, p. 11).

4. Student-Teacher Strains

Adults bring a wide inventory of experience with them to learning. As a result, they do not automatically accord expertise to their teachers, but elect to appraise the knowledge an instructor disseminates against their own frame of reference to make a critical assessment of that person's fitness to facilitate learning. When this fails to happen, the adult learner objects:

I do not stand for less than respect from teachers and instructional personnel and am not nearly as intimidated as I was at a younger age. Now, I don't necessarily believe everything that faculty say and teach and am not afraid to question their answers.

A 26-year-old female added: "I have also encountered professors whom I seriously question why and how they are teaching."

Her observation provides a perfect segue into another often articulated belief by adult students that faculty appear to employ different standards in evaluating the academic performance of differently aged learners. One respondent, age 44, claimed that these ostensibly arbitrary expectations place an added layer of stress on older students already coping with heightened self-doubt:

I feel that the faculty have two sets of rules for adults and the younger students. They expect more from the adult student even though most of us hold down full-time jobs and manage families. . . . For most of us adults, this is our last chance for an education; the younger students are just beginning their adult lives. I know for myself it takes a longer time to read and retain the material. Faculty need to keep these things in mind.

By way of corollary, a 39-year-old African-American male continued with this same theme: "The adult student, having sacrificed time from family and leisure, if any, expects more from the professor . . . feeling that the professor works for him."

In yet another angle on this issue, one respondent noted: "I also have experienced that professors tend not to be lenient when it comes to homework. Some are not keen to the idea that homework may not get done due to a child being ill. It's tough being a parent and a student." There were numerous instances where respondents recalled conflicts with faculty over assignment deadlines and how intractable teachers were in granting extensions or resolving problems. This student-mother of three recounts the anger she felt when her request for help was rejected:

Their (faculty) feelings: If you're having trouble, too bad! Can't keep up, too bad! Need tutoring, not my problem! They make you feel like a second-class citizen if you are an adult. My friend was told: "You've got to choose: is it going to be your family or school?"

Teaching techniques also emerged as a point of contention for adult students. Lectures consistently failed to ignite passions. Intellectual stimulation and growth rarely developed from the taking of notes.

Adults expressed a strong preference for the interactive, the contextual, the faciliatory. Faculty need to do more than just read notes from past lectures. They need to get adults involved or else they risk losing their interest. If at all possible, teachers should find ways of linking course content with concrete examples which might actually accelerate the learning process whenever the two are integrated.

5. Organizational Obstacles

Perhaps the first and last line of resistance to nontraditional students is the academic organization and the culture it spawns: static, impersonal, indifferent. As expected, academic bureaucracy continues to peeve adult students who admonish colleges for their unresponsiveness to the needs of an older clientele (Wingard, 1995). To date, the modifications universities have made to accommodate adults are piecemeal and concessionary: expanding an evening schedule of classes, extending lab and library hours, or adding weekend noncredit or nondegree programs. Even now, the majority of degree-oriented academic programs still require full-time residency, or at least a schedule capable of reserving entire afternoons or mornings.

I am writing through the eyes of an adult, white, female, age 26. I am a mother, wife, and a student. I have encountered several obstacles that I feel are biased towards adults who are students.
   The first is: In order to enter the Nursing program, I had to resign from a high paying job that was paying for school and take a part-time evening job. The major obstacle is that college curriculums and schedules are not geared toward working adult students.

Predictably, when peoples' livelihoods are compromised by organizational inflexibility, an all too common occurrence for many adult students, the student-institutional relationship suffers lasting damage. At such a point, conditions conducive to learning will be nearly impossible to foster.
   The chorus of protests grew louder when adults discussed the difficulties they encountered in using campus support services, from counseling appointments to bookstore hours. One summarized her frustration:

Times that services are offered are also a problem. Many of the offices and services (like the bookstore—I can't stop back 3 or four times per week—I work *every* day that I'm not in school) are not open when I could have access to them. I've had trouble being able to see an advisor, or even talk to one about a problem or question that I have concerning school.

This respondent was perplexed and angered by disservice of a different sort.

The first day I came to UC to register for classes, the woman at registration informed that since I would not be able to get into the College of Education I might as well just come back next quarter. I almost fell over. I said that I needed to take classes NOW. . . . (Later) I found the director of my program who walked me through registration in the College of Education without any hassles.

Another batch of replies revolved around the treatment adults received from university personnel. Primary areas of concern for adults was staff inability to make referrals to more specialized resources, limited knowledge of broader university policies outside their departments, or, in some cases, insufficient expertise in the functional area staff members served in. Alluding to interactions with professional staff, one respondent said in a sweeping indictment: "I feel they are all very unhelpful. I doubt they care at all about the adult student." Another student was more particular:

I have been very discouraged, disheartened, and on one occasion very angry at the lack of knowledge that advisors in the financial aid department have to share with students. In my husband's case, their lack of knowledge forced him to go back to work (without his degree) after 15 years of hard work and determination.

Yet the financial aid office was not the only place at which their dissatisfaction was directed. Adult students cited additional institutional structures that grieve them, such as the scarcity of cocurricular opportunities catering to adult and evening students. Everything from student activities through in/externship programs seems specifically designed for younger students. One respondent took offense at this pattern: "In my experience, younger students take ski trips sponsored by the college or have opportunities to visit local companies. I have never been able to participate in any of these or other activities because there was no one to watch my daughter."

Also, there were two respondents who mentioned the lack of accommodation in campus and classroom facilities. An older student, age 49, made critical remarks about the facilities adult students are asked to adapt to, including classroom chairs "more accommodating" to younger bodies, the lower lighting necessary when overhead projectors are used as instructional aids in class, and the "difficulties in stair climbing" for adults suffering from age-related infirmities.

While the reader may find a shred of eccentricity in these last impressions, adults find much in the institutional ambiance to trouble them (O'Connor, 1994). Based on what we have heard in these accounts and others, it is not an exaggeration to assert that unhappiness over the manner in which college culture and systems treat adult students sometimes reach a level where leaving campus sometimes seems the only honorable retreat for adult students.

RELATED ISSUES AND CONCERNS

A significant number of adult students raised the issue of commitment to learning, particularly as demonstrated by younger students. Eight of twenty-six actually mentioned the word "serious" in describing their approach and faulting younger students for lacking it. This concern was elaborated upon in the "student-to-student tension" section, where adults consistently commented on the all-too-casual attitude of younger students toward class attendance, participation, and assignments, identifying it as a primary source of agitation between the groups. More than a few of the adults surveyed were incredulous over some of the reasons younger students cited for neglecting academic responsibilities, such as poor weather, the need to sleep, or excessive night life. As one respondent reacted after overhearing two teenage students complain about going to class on the first warm day of spring: "The mother in me just wanted to shake the one girl and say 'I don't think your parents would like spending thousands of dollars on your tuition knowing you plan to skip out on class to sun yourself today.'"

Another interesting observation was the "rush" adult students derived from academic success. A female student, age 29, declared:

I never would have believed the excitement you feel when grades come out without actually experiencing it. It is a reward that can't be compared to a paycheck—it is knowledge that you are bettering yourself for your lifetime.

Finally, I cannot refrain from quoting from the reply received from the one nonadult (recall that 25 of 26 surveys were from respondents 22 and older) female in the class that provided survey participants. Her perception of adult classmates and her relationship to them was touching:

I realize it is difficult to come back to school after years off, but I think problems can affect both of us. Being younger than most people here, I feel I'm not always taken seriously. I don't consider myself to be super intelligent but I have lived and seen things in my life. No one can judge or know your experiences and I'm very serious about school. . . . You make decisions in your life and you have to live with them.

Wisdom comes from unexpected places, and this 20-year old was one such delightful surprise. Perhaps in the haste to affirm and accredit the voice of older students on an institutional level, we discount the individual in the class who is unlike the majority, whatever age, race, gender, or ethnicity they may be. Marginalization appears to be the inevitable fate of any person who is different from the crowd. This is an important lesson and one revisited throughout this book.

DISCUSSION

To assure a degree of integrity in reporting these findings, it must be duly noted that within these new stories of struggle there were many complimentary and commendable things said by respondents about professors, support services, and their younger colleagues. The praise was especially plentiful on what adults generally thought of their teachers. In at least a handful of cases, students expressed appreciation for the respect instructors showed them, believing it could be attributed to faculty seeing how much more they invested in learning compared to traditional students. Further, a sizable number indicated that their professors were understanding of the unique issues adults faced in trying to balance schoolwork with family problems like sick children. Finally, the criticisms they made against younger classmates were frequently softened with sighs that in their own youth they would have been equally preoccupied with the social rather than intellectual aspects of college life.

The data collected in this study surpassed expectations on several counts. First, it let adult students self-identify areas where differences and difficulties existed. Interestingly, they listed hardships of economic, social, psychological, and cultural dimensions, unknowingly substantiating the assumption of critical theory that resistance to nonmajority populations takes multiple forms within the academic organization. Second, comments were presented in the words of respondents, thus allowing an additional and illuminating layer of metaphor to come through in the language they used to recount struggles. Paraphrasing, no matter how gifted the author, cannot begin to portray the same drama. It is only through the idiom of the experiencer that we might understand the pathos of their trials, as postmodernism predicts. Finally, there was a significant level of continuity in the type of problems students mentioned as endangering educational persistence. We can at least partially explain this as the result of the survey's format and question design. Still, the coincidence of responses identifying similar experiences of struggle was unexpected, if not remarkable.

Too many times, educators rely on nonrepresentative student sources to take the campus pulse and in the process lose sight of wider concerns. College presidents and deans are especially prone to such malfeasance, assuming that the chair of the interfraternity council or the elected officers of student government can speak for all students. On today's multicultural campuses, nothing could be farther from reality. Impressions, anecdotal or direct, sought only from student leaders or activists, inevitably create an "unbalanced picture" (Sandeen, 1991, p. 41) and can lead to grave miscalculations on the part of faculty and administration in gauging student opinions.

My professional life at an open-access community college of an urban university may serve as an example of some value. For in spite of abundant claims in the literature that adults are goal-centered, credential-conscious, and task-driven to the exclusion of all else in the broader academic picture, I have witnessed a far different scenario.

The acting president of our student government association is a 36-year-old male who left the fast track at Unisys Corporation to return to his real passion—helping people through a career in the medical arts. Lest the reader think him an exception, let me mention a few others. One of the most gifted "counselors" in our Disability Services office attending to the needs of physically and cognitively disabled students is a 48-year-old mother of three who regularly enrolls for a full-time load each quarter and still works more than thirty-five hours per week in that office. In 1995 our annual Student of the Year award honoring academic and college service excellence went to a licensed practical nurse and mother of two. "Karen" is 42. Suffice it to say, these individuals are *not* unusual here and fairly represent our college's student body. It is my contention that adult students and their unselfish willingness to make a difference extends beyond my little corner of academia.

The moral is clear: adults dedicated to learning, and aware that it occurs formally and casually, *create* time to contribute to academic endeavors they see as worthwhile. Though many of my colleagues might disagree, mature students consciously seek out issues and activities where their talents can be applied for the good of others. When issues revolve around politics, raising concerns in matters of organizational leadership, they become even more interested. Theory, the critical and postmodern varieties, enlightens us to the possibility that students interact with ideas and test values on terrain radically different from what pedagogues and administrators anticipate. It is at the nexus of these theories that educators might look for new approaches to studying adult students and their commitment to the entire learning enterprise.

SUMMARY

The survey administered was not created to objective or quantitative specifications. Consistent with a critical theory that aspires to reclaim the discourses of the marginalized, my desire was to capture the thoughts and feelings of adults in their own voices by providing enough direction in the questionnaire so that responses did not drift. That this much has been accomplished, I am confident.

As to the results of this investigation, if they are not conclusive, they are at least instructive of how adult students perceive their social, economic, and cultural selves in relation to the university. The views they shared, describing sensations of vulnerability, anger, and even resignation about the resistance facing them, awakens us to the possibilities of critical and postmodern theories as more than frameworks for interpretation. They permitted the reader to see how these theoretical paradigms could provide the insights necessary to creating an entirely new academic milieu in which all forms of opposition, concealed and overt, to an adult presence have been eliminated.

Consequently I regard my findings as helpful for what they fail to point out, as well as for what they offer in supporting claims of anti-adult institutional biases. For it seems that students, even older ones, are as thoroughly indoctrinated into the culture of schooling as younger peers. They are not always trained, as critical theorists advocate, to "critically interrogate and authenticate" (Aronowitz and Giroux, 1991) their own circumstances in socially constructed settings such as the college. Adults also retain an innocent trust in social institutions parented by the dominant culture. Yet there is a strand of wariness threading its way through their personal narratives. Almost all acknowledge some feeling of "Otherness," or alienation, from mainstream campus culture. This appears particularly strong for those who have been away from the classroom for a number of years.

Does this anthology of personal stories of hardship suggest that higher education remains unsympathetic to the needs of the adult learner? Are these tales convincing evidence that academic intolerance continues to greet mature students entering college? Can we project from these accounts that adults remain "at-risk" throughout the landscape of higher education?

Perhaps not. It does not really matter. This study was not designed to so overwhelm the scales that the reader could no longer deny the persistence of organizational inertia on the part of colleges or cultural prohibitions functioning to marginalize adult students. Regardless of personal interest, I make no pretensions to the universality of my discoveries.

It is the sublime, the unaccentuated, the unspoken in the words of the students that concern me. Subtlety reveals more than declaration. Feeling tells as much as fact. And nuance, simple or symbolic, is the most enlightening of all. If the reader carefully reviews the excerpts from the students who contributed to this chapter, I believe he or she will be affected the same way I was. Through the mists of each tale, bits of deprivation and sacrifice shine through. These adults are not living off the wealth of indulgent parents, nor are they living lavishly through student financial aid as some educators are wont to suggest. The majority struggle to locate funds to continue their education, usually resorting to a fragile balance of family support, income from work, and some slight student loan or grant assistance. Most important, they are persisting. Despite feelings of disempowerment, adult students are not easily discouraged. Personal ambitions motivate them, as does a yearning to keep abreast of an internal clock that informs them time may not be so limitless as it once seemed. For a few, there is a personal realization that this may be one of the last chances to finish a task they started decades earlier.

What survives in the stories of these students is the stuff of legends. Taken individually, these stories stand as testimony to transcendence. Collectively, their discourse is vibrant with re-forming identities, alternative readings of social and economic reality, and candid criticism of academic culture from the perspective of someone on the margins looking in.

Chapter 5

Postmodern Possibilities in Adult Education

> At issue here is the development of a pedagogy that replaces the authoritative language of recitation with an approach that allows students to speak from their own histories, collective memories, and voices while simultaneously challenging the grounds on which knowledge and power are constructed and legitimated.
> —H. Giroux, "Border Pedagogy in the Age of Postmodernism"

Philosophically considered, society cannot exist apart from human beings who en masse assume responsibility for its construction. Conversely, it is generally accepted that individuals are primarily formed by society and socializing processes. Is it possible that a synthesis can be deduced from such apparently conflicting premises? If indeed we all participate in the creation of the social world and therefore are its architects, how is it that we have since largely become subjugated to a reality that did not exist except through our handiwork? A potential reply comes from postmodern theory when it proposes that persons and society "exist in a state of continuous construction and reconstruction" (Gergen, 1991, p. 6).

An analogy arises in the tale of adult educators and adult education programs. They, too, found themselves beholden to an edifice that grew to eclipse its designers. Purposes were debated, programs created, and colleges built to house them, all of which flourished under institutional nurturing. Unfortunately, academic organizations that pledged to cultivate the intellectual talents and gifts of people without preference now exert the same control over students as social convention does over members of society. In both social and educational domains, people were somehow forgotten in modernism's hunger for progress only to reemerge as servants of monolithic structures rather than masters. All but the most naively idealistic among us would concede that colleges now overshadow the individual students they were intended to serve. One student, or educator, trying to change the academy faces an almost hopeless task.

Regrettably, educational institutions seem highly impervious to attacks made against their less humane aspects. Since internal commitment to egalitarianism was always more myth than reality (Milner, 1972), universities formed esoteric, insular cultures of their own. With community members bound together by an ideology, these academic enclaves developed a sense of solidarity and privilege (Cohen, 1993). Authority and prestige became the bailiwick of the faculty, competition and competency the lot of students. How we might break this unfortunate cycle and restore humanity to the impersonal aura colleges adopted in the era of late capitalism (Jameson, 1991) is our central concern.

This essay addresses how higher education might rethink its culture and adapt its practices to better meet contemporary instead of archaic objectives in adult education. Yvonna Lincoln (1991) concludes, after an extensive review of the literature on leadership and students, that higher education researchers still have not addressed the question of why select individuals and groups are exiled to the "margins of academe." She speculates, however, that neglect of such a disturbing possibility stems from scholars' reluctance to acknowledge bias within academic culture.

A number of fundamental issues related to both teaching and learning outcomes will be taken apart and then reassembled, hoping that their reconstruction along terms kinder to the discourse of adult Otherness prompts change. To do this, the reader will be introduced to postmodern theory and acquire a working knowledge of its concepts and assumptions, enabling more in-depth study to occur in subsequent sections. Like its cousin, critical theory, postmodernism is adept at "mining the contradictory and oppositional insights" (Aronowitz and Giroux, 1991, p. 62) central to a radically transformative educational project. Dialectically, we will consider philosophical and functional areas of adult education that are predisposed to self-contradiction (Gumport, 1991) with the purpose of synthesizing new solutions. Optimally, our discoveries will abet rather than impede the democratic aims of higher education.

To accomplish this task, we will explore several topics affecting the nature and practice of adult education. Foremost, we will spend some time examining the work of Knowles and other prominent adult educators to see where andragogical science intersects with and might be enhanced by postmodern possibility. The middle portion of this chapter will consider past, present, and future postmodern experiments in adult education. This will be followed by the outlining of an adult academic program that builds upon border andragogy and praxis learning, two concepts crucial to the postmodern educational project.

THE POSTMODERN CONDITION

An appropriate place to begin presents itself in postmodern theory and its origins. Bagnall (1995) helps illuminate the linkage between modern and postmodern eras and thought:

Postmodernity is a transformative, disruptive cultural change from a modernist epoch to a postmodern one. It incorporates but *problematizes* [italics added] modernity—the scientific, industrial, and social programs, institutions, actions, and artifacts generated by the humanistic and Enlightenment search for the universal foundations of truth, morality, and aesthetics—*in pursuit of human emancipation* [italics added]." (p. 81)

Postmodernism questions the inherited social, political, aesthetic, and psychological "verities" of modernity. What it says, simply, is that modernist truths are insufficient representations of current reality or, at the very least, provide only one limited version of it. Additionally, postmodernism assaults the legacy of modernism, uncovering the illogic in, for example, its advocacy of science and technology as a means to bettering the human condition while during this same period both did very little to curb poverty, depravity, or war, all of which persisted on an unprecedented scale throughout the "civilized" world. In the same vein, postmodernism takes issue with modernity's exalting of reason as the summit of human interaction, contending that Romanticism's noble sentiment of man's natural goodness (Smith, 1990) and the Enlightenment's trust in man's capacity to use reason benevolently cannot be sustained under the microscope of history. The twentieth century, with its wild swings of political, social, and religious fanaticism leading to massive human repression and destruction, is offered as an exhibit of modernism's failures.

Declaring its opposition to much of what has been handed down for centuries as academic canon, that amalgamation of great books and master narratives from Plato through Marx as they lay the foundation of liberal education and the classic curriculum (Poster, 1989; Rosemary, 1991), postmodernism outrages the pedants among us. Distilled down to its essence, this discourse tells us that human history as recorded and retold is unfinished in its "ethnocentric equation of history with the triumphs of Western Civilization" (Giroux, 1988b, p. 162). As presently recounted, history discounts the voices, thoughts, and stories of all but a select few whose iconoclastic status in Western culture remains sacred. Postmodern theory muses not so much upon denigrating the values of European culture as much as it does on putting them in honest perspective while concurrently crediting the discourses of peripheral groups and their own unique versions of history and truth. Kenneth Gergen stresses this notion in *The Saturated Self: Dilemmas of Identity in Contemporary Life* (1991): "The postmodern condition is more generally marked by a plurality of voices vying for the right to reality—to be accepted as legitimate expressions of the true and the good. As the voices expand in power and presence, all that seemed proper, right-minded and well understood is subverted" (p. 6). For it is in these other representations—arising from lives of struggle and experiences of oppression—that a fuller and poignant reading of the human experience is rendered.

Socially, postmodernism is an intrepid celebration and legitimation of difference (Bannet, 1993). Previously excluded, alternative ways of being and perceiving have suddenly been validated in recompense for past suppression imposed by obedience to the dominant culture. Further, postmodernism arises as a centrifugal force (Kellner, 1989), the outward momentum we now observe in the fracturing of social formations like the family, the degeneration of political debate into factional agenda-ism, and proliferation of extremist views on a plethora of public policy issues from abortion to welfare, making one wonder if the multitude of differences are ever capable of being bridged. Of course, it is the unapologetic proclamation of disintegration (Dews, 1987), this turbulent unraveling of the social fabric, that earns postmodernism the unqualified enmity of modernists. For in these cultural convulsions they detect the old order wavering and their positions in it becoming more tenuous. Threatening or not, depending on one's perspective, the concussions splintering our social landscape are plentiful and real.

Such symptoms also seem to suggest a devolution or, at best, a lapsing of mass consciousness to the stimulus-rich but meaning- devoid existence in which we find ourselves. Resultingly, agreement and action upon shared civic principles—gestures crucial to democracy—may be irrevocably lost in the postmodern age. Increasingly spellbound by simulacra (Baudrillard, 1994)—the stream of vicarious simulations fed to us in television's messages or in cyberspace's computer screens—we see our world transformed into a hollow one, dissociated from meaning and unsure about reality. A key assertion of postmodernism concerns the dissolution of meaning since reality can no longer be demarcated, but becomes porous and shifting under the flood of images, signs, and symbols overwhelming people each day.

Whereas before social interaction was a source of communality and personal pleasure, people now elect to "retreat into their electronic castles" (Bennis, 1989, p. 41) at the end of the workday, bidding farewell to their neighbors and the world as the automatic garage door whirs mechanically closed. Such a tableau reveals postmodernism's more antisocial elements and how the self is becoming increasingly decentered (Tierney, 1993), disconnecting individuals from the social and cultural tapestry that held modernity's "melting pot" society together. Still, it is illustrative of the antisocial barriers students and teachers must overcome in a common search for meaning.

Finally, postmodernism, as a politics of pluralistic inclusion, gives the most lucid insights in charting a new course for democracy. Modernity's maxim that democracy is served through majority rule (Cianciolo, 1995) went the way of the dinosaur in postmodern politics. It is unrelenting in its insistence upon a multiplicity of social positions, doubts they can be reconciled through the facade of voting, and scoffs at democracy's claim that the needs of those on the margin are looked after by those at the center of power. As Fox (1995, p. 11) notes, within the postmodern "discourse we can expect a struggle over meanings; we expect argumentation, claiming, and counterclaiming, not harmonious consensus" as diverse individuals try to negotiate through difference. Academically, it informs us that higher education erred in the blind transmission of select enculturated ideologies (e.g., Western, capitalistic) and the perpetuation of highly exclusionary, parochial practices designed to preserve them. For the last two centuries, universities were accessible to only the few, politically viable groups deemed so by student and professorial cadres. The colonial college served precisely that end—to reproduce traditional American political and social systems and power structures (Rudolph, 1962). Postmodernists assert that justice might be done in atoning for a cavalier past by admitting its lingering injustices and, through spirited and uncompromising debate, forging a multicultural coalition for change (ACSCU-WASC, 1994).

Fragmentation and disintegration. Disparate ways of knowing and multiple meanings in language and perception. Specific, partial, localized instead of master histories. Personal and subcultural tellings over universal truths. Reality growing thinner while a delusional "hyperreality" (Baudrillard, 1988) encroaches upon us. If such are some of the nuances of the postmodern condition, what do they portend for education, specifically higher education and the adult?

In spite of some unsettling aspects, postmodernism still inspires a ray of hope. Educationally, it warns that traditional models of teaching, learning, and organizational structure are ineffectual on today's campus (O'Toole, 1995). It teases us to try something a little more daring, to revisit the foundations of adult learning with an open mind. Hierarchical paradigms in the classroom must give way to collaboration. Professor as omniscient authority figure must surrender to teacher as co-learner, discussion facilitator, and affirmer of student experience as a basis for learning. All the previous ingredients in the customary mix for adult education are subject to postmodern reinterpretation. The forthcoming narrative should prove intellectually provocative and challenge the reader to reconsider his or her own notions of adult education.

EXTENDING ANDRAGOGY THROUGH POSTMODERN THEORY

That adults come to college with very different expectations and needs from younger students has been abundantly documented (Dewey, 1916; Lindeman, 1926; Grattan, 1959; Apps, 1981; Heerman, Enders, and Wine, 1980; Cross, 1981; Knox, 1986; Cervero, 1988; Jackson, 1995). Few with any exposure to adult education research would dispute this statement. But apart from returning to former discussions and rehashing tired ideas, what are we really talking about?

Over the last two decades a wealth of research has been published on adult education and the budding science of andragogy. The term *andragogy* was introduced by a Dutch professor in 1951 and soon became common parlance in European universities. Its use by American educators was relatively recent, with Malcolm Knowles' introduction of it in 1970 in *The Modern Practice of Adult Education: Andragogy versus Pedagogy*. In this and subsequent works (1984,

1990, 1995), Knowles supplies a detailed description of andragogy and examines its unique properties. For our analysis, they will be revisited here.

The Five Principles of Andragogy

1. The learner is self-directed.
2. Adults enter into education with a wealth and variety of experiences younger students do not have.
3. Adults are psychologically more ready to learn than traditional-age students.
4. Adults bring a life-centered, task-oriented, experience-informed orientation to learning.
5. Adults are *internally* motivated to learn. (Knowles, 1984, pp. 9–12)

Our present focus rests not on the letter of these basic principles as much as on their spirit. Properly invoked for their conceptual capacities, they inspire suggestions for designing an optimal learning environment for adults. Postmodern theory permits a reinterpretion of andragogy's fundamentals to fit the robustly mosaic culture that defines contemporary higher education. Adults, as befits culturally disadvantaged student cohorts, are naturally central to this vision. Bearing this premise in mind, let us briefly explore the tenets of andragogy through a postmodern lens.

1. The Learner Is Self-Directed

Self-directed activity is the core of andragogy. This direction emerges from a wellspring deep in the psychology of adults. As Knowles suggests, adults' self-awareness that they need to learn something more (1990, p. 57) provides a compelling urge to seek out educational opportunity. Younger students attend college for an assortment of reasons that are usually externally driven—parents. Older students enroll because of this inner drive to grow through knowing. An expansion of this notion is found in mature students who demonstrate the ability to make reasonable and informed choices regarding the content and context of learning. Thus their input would be essential in determining various components of the educational process—curriculum, instructional style, and setting.

Postmodernism takes a different view of self-directedness, as it challenges the modernist assumption of individuals as free and autonomous. Doubting the ability of the individual to act freely and according to his or her own will, which conveniently neglects the influence of social control over personal freedom, postmodernism posits an alternative view. Emphasis is placed more on the "embeddedness of individual identity within the various discourses through which each person has acted and is acting" (Bagnall, 1995, p. 85). All of us, inextricable from the cultural and social spheres we travel between in living, are both "molded and fragmented" by these different discourses. Inasmuch as an adult student has acquired an awareness of the multiple, concurrent dramas in which they play simultaneous roles, self-directedness in learning remains a possibility. However, it is critical for students and educators alike to comprehend the many different social, political, and cultural variables converging to impact upon and occasionally inhibit the learning process.

2. The Role of Experience

Another fundamental proposition of andragogy concerns the role of experience in adult learning. Adults "enter into educational activity with a greater volume and a different quality of experience from youth" (Knowles, 1984, p. 10). This breadth of volume comes with age. Quality of experience refers to the range and mixture of roles adults assume: parent, spouse, accountant, student. Therefore, adults commence with a broader frame of reference for learning. But Knowles does not stop there. Adult students also value the experiences of *other* older students as staples for class discussion and exploration. Hence the effective educator of adults will place a "greater emphasis on experiential techniques. . . over transmittal techniques" (1990, p. 59).

Postmodernism envelops this same experiential base in a discourse, epistemology, or "way of knowing" that presupposes a particular worldview (Tisdell, 1993a). Discourses exist at individual, group, and subcultural levels. Across each layer, they represent a shared set of assumptions, beliefs, and conversations that impart a unique perspective to the beholder. They also provide a common context with which most adults are familiar, having passed through similar developmental tasks that students lesser in years have not had the opportunity to cope with. This communality of domestic and career experiences combined with a yearning to build upon prior knowledge coalesce into a feeling that binds adult students together.

3. Adults Are Psychologically More Ready to Learn

Based on what we know of cognitive developmental psychology (e.g., the works of Piaget, Perry, Kohlberg, and Gilligan), Knowles posits that adults search out educational opportunity when something in their personal life triggers a fresh, acute need to know. Knowles says that number of catalysts exist, but identifies among the "chief sources of readiness" (1984, p. 11) for additional education job loss, divorce, marriage, death of a spouse or relative, or birth of children. The constant that cuts across all these potential contributors to learning readiness is a dramatic change in personal circumstances, usually in the form of a rite of passage to the next chapter of life.

Critical theory refers to this preparedness to learn in adults as *consciencization* (Freire, 1972a). Underlying it is an inevitable heightening of consciousness of self in relation to society. Through the course of living and learning, adults continuously revisit their value systems at times of internal or external crisis. Reevaluation of beliefs typically happens at moments of dissonance or disjuncture (Jarvis, 1987), when the adult encounters a problem that s/he is cognitively unequipped to resolve. During these unsettling intervals of introspection, the revelation comes that they are deficient in a critical area of knowledge or that intellectual skills obtained years earlier need expanding. Usually in the midst of or shortly after the disjunctures, adults make the decision to return to the classroom and acquire new cognitive tools.

4. Adults Bring a Life-Centered, Task-Oriented Approach to Learning

Adult educators have long known that mature learners prefer a practical approach to learning (Cross, 1981). Understanding what it takes to survive in the world independently, adults approach learning activities with pragmatic motives. Cognizant of this, educators should employ instructional methods that rely heavily on group discussion and concrete examples (Wlodkowski, 1985, p. 18) to connect formal learning to everyday life. For, just as they have learned to do in resolving personal, family, or career problems, adult students rely on a "rich reservoir of experience" (Knowles, 1984) to assist them in problem solving.

Postmodern educators identify the agency of living as enhancing learning. Here "agency" means the stuff of daily life—interactions, obstacles, and successes—as contributing to the formation of a personal identity and paradigm (Aronowitz and Giroux, 1991). In contrast to detractors of experiential learning, postmodernists contend that "everyday" as learning substance is far more useful than the homogenized curricula taught in formal educational programs that represent a solitary, albeit lionized, Westernized intellectual tradition. The growth

potential in the diverse vignettes of living cannot be artificially replicated in the classroom and makes life-centered learning the most
appropriate avenue in adult education.

5. Adults Are Internally Motivated to Learn

This principle distinguishes older students from younger counterparts who are often enrolled in college because of social and parental
pressures (Apps, 1981). Adults also have a clearer, better-defined
self-concept which usually includes a values set that prizes educational
activity (Knowles, 1984, p. 9) over less worthwhile pursuits. For their
part, adults enter the university for reasons almost entirely internalized
(Knowles, 1990, p. 63). Factors often cited for their return to college
include the desire for a higher quality of life, enhancing self-esteem, or
to give something back as an educated person to the community,
culture, and society of which they are members. Unlike youthful peers,
adults study because they have a genuine interest in growth and
development rather than because it is a family expectation.

Postmodernism offers another rationale for why adults are internally
motivated to continue their education. It emerges in the principle of
praxis, or reflective learning as a prerequiste to informed action (Willets,
Boyce, and Franklin, 1995). Acquainted firsthand with the inequality
rampant in the world, some adults have reached a phase of psychosocial
development where they long to make a difference, to contribute in
various ways to the betterment of all persons, especially those residing
on the margins. According to psychologists, as we age, this desire to
transcend personal and social limitations becomes so insistent that
adults must find an outlet in which to channel their intellectual energies.
Education, as the price of admission into the debate over public policy
and as a precursor to social activism, seems a natural place to start.

For some time, educators of adults have felt pressure either to align
themselves with the andragogical movement or to remain steadfast
disciples of pedagogy. As pedagogy is viewed as having a content-driven
approach to learning and andragogy a life-centered orientation, some
have argued that their differences are irreconcilable. The tendency
toward allying with one or the other school may in fact be unnecessary.
In an article challenging this popular assumption, Delahaye, Limerick,
and Hearn (1994) claim that these methods need not be mutually
exclusive but share the same fundamental concerns in key areas. Support of one does not imply an abandonment of the other. Moreover,
this research team concluded that the most accomplished teachers of

adults are those who recognize the axes of intersection and work from an internal mental construct that proceeds with elements of both.

POSTMODERN EXPERIMENTS—PAST AND PRESENT

Adult education has drawn the interest of sociologists and educators for many years. Significant scholarship on the school-to-society relationship exists (Paterson, 1979; Peters, 1980; Brookfield, 1985, 1986; Jarvis, 1987a, 1987b; Jones, 1988) and would require considerable amounts of time to examine thoroughly. Much of what has been written about adult education from a sociological concern pertains to the democratizing of society. Equality, justice, and mobility are frequently highlighted in discussions on the link between higher education and the social outcomes.

If postmodernism is perhaps the purest and most radical abstraction of democracy, it shows educators the pluralistic potential yet contained in formal learning. It manages this by probing the cultural rituals of academic institutions at various levels of encounter and criticizes democracy for silencing the voices of marginal peoples and their histories (Welton, 1993) in shaping the human condition. How can a complete and representative picture of the contemporary world be sketched when the knowledge informing it omits the tellings of those whose struggles remind us of a not-too-distant past where selective and mass oppression still prevailed? It is, after all, in this ultimately human experience of struggle and sorrow that different persons arrive at a common place and are drawn closer together, if only for a moment. Democracy can bear that name only when the society that embraces it encourages a public airing of disparate, suppressed, and localized (Lyotard, 1984) viewpoints not widely known across our polity. Higher education, as a social institution pledged to intellectual freedom, must engender the same opportunity.

Postmodernism questions the authority of established disciplines on the grounds that they suffer from intellectual narrowness and that their teachings are historically relevant primarily to the past eras that hatched them. Giroux (1988b, p. 163) extends this argument: "There is no tradition or story that can speak with authority and certainty for all of humanity." This observation resonates with the scholar in all of us, knowing from anthropology, for instance, the absurdity of projecting a cosmology of, say, one sub-Saharan tribe to European or Asian peoples, much less to all humankind and passing it off as absolute truth. When we apply such critical logic to Western science, however, mur-

murs of protest begin to arise. It is a wonder to examine the bigotry still carried in our intellectual traditions.

Additionally, postmodernism declares the traditional student-faculty relationship to be antithetical to learning because significant differences in the power and autonomy are meted to each, with the edge clearly favoring the teacher. A student recently recalled the vacant feeling he was left with from interaction of this kind: "The basic relationship between students and faculty is that we listen and they talk" (Tierney, 1989, p. 92). This outdated picture of the teacher-student relationship withers under postmodern scrutiny. In its view, students and teachers must come together as co-inquirers and persuade each other to test assumptions and reexamine values about the nature of knowledge. In particular, the experiences of adults are interrogated and critically evaluated for their educational aspects and become the primary material for class discussion.

Finally, postmodernism denies the preeminence of academic canon on the grounds that it categorically ignores alternative theories, explanations, and readings (e.g., "herstories") originating from persons and groups subordinate to the dominant culture. As a result, it "rejects the European tradition as the exclusive referent for what is historical, cultural, and political truth" (Giroux, 1988b). Further, postmodernism contends that the real stuff of learning, of human transcendence, can emerge from the largely ignored stories of these oppressed peoples as their stories are the product of more direct encounter and reflection rather than simply conveyed from prior generations.

Schools and colleges, as sites of cultural enactment, replicate our intellectual heritage across generations. We thus, prima facie, grant that the dominant culture is preserved and social continuity assured. Forgotten in this admission remains the fact that the body of knowledge transmitted, if prejudices or exclusions exist, persists with these flaws rather than being purged. Nonetheless, proud of its role in cultural reproduction, higher education employs mechanisms—a standard curriculum, content-driven instruction, and so on—to protect the process of transmission and typically avoids actions that might betray this mission. Perhaps this is why the university ignores calls to change and innovation. Fortunately, the postmodern tide is swelling and soon to immerse these islets of resistance. The signs surround us, and history makes it inevitable. "We are living in a transitional era in which emerging social conditions call into question the ability of old orthodoxies to name and understand the changes that are ushering us into the twenty-first century" (Aronowitz and Giroux, 1991, p. 66).

Yet educational experiments of postmodern import occurred even during the golden age of modernity. The Antigonish Movement that flowered at St. Frances Xavier College under Moses Coady, a Jesuit priest, in 1940s Canada was certainly ahead of its time in recognizing the transformative potential present in adult education as it blended education with ethics and a program of social justice (Laidlaw, 1961). Unlike so many, Moses Coady could "not abandon the poor of his generation to a life without hope of improvement. . . . He chose instead, to work directly and immediately with adults in economic need" (Crane, 1987, p. 229). The philosophy of the Antigonish Movement was built upon six assumptions, which obviously antedate but bear uncanny resemblance to postmodern ideas: (1) one must assert the primacy of the individual; (2) social reform must come through education; (3) education must begin with and speak to economic need; (4) education is enhanced through group action; (5) lasting changes in social institutions (including schools and colleges) must precede social reform; and (6) the ultimate objective of adult education is a full, autonomous life for everyone in the community. In these principles, one discerns themes of inclusion, individual and group empowerment, and social and economic advancement through education.

More recently the Universidad Popular (UP) in Chicago surfaced as another postmodern experiment in higher education. This project arose from disillusionment in the city's Latino neighborhoods over a public postsecondary system that failed to attract, address, and retain Hispanic adults. Undeterred by a lack of funding at its inception, the Universidad took up residence between a taco restaurant and a community health clinic, heralding its opening through signs placed in a "narrow storefront." Quoting Heaney (1989, p. 3), who chronicled this formative period, the UP

survived nine tumultuous years of struggle between the Latino community and the City Colleges of Chicago. The issue over which they fought was community control. Several organizations contributed to its beginning. An educational philosophy and purpose began to emerge from a variety of adult education classes long before the concept of a community center had developed.

As another commentator notes, to be effective, learning must be tied to experiences within a spectrum of encounter familiar to the student population being served (Jeria, 1990, p. 96). It must necessarily involve the struggles and lessons of daily life and allow students the opportunity to take action on issues of local origin, which is precisely what UP did. Community-inspired educational experiments such as the UP offer visible proof of postmodernism's claim that marginalized groups, once awakened to systematic hegemony, will seize the initiative and reclaim the intellectual space denied them in traditional higher education.

Perhaps the most vivid postmodern incarnation of adult education can be found in the alternative, interdisciplinary model espoused by the Union Institute in Cincinnati, Ohio. Although this region of the country is not renowned for pioneering radical educational projects, the Union has nearly perfected a self-directed scheme for adult education. In its modulations—philosophical, structural and interpersonal—the Union is styled upon postmodern architecture. The following observations are based on my four-year tenure in their administration, the Graduate School Application booklet, and the Graduate School *Blue Book* (catalog), as well as personal experiences while enrolled as a Ph.D. "learner."

Philosophically, the Union permits adult learners to bring to education distinct portfolios of experiences every bit as valuable as knowledge acquired in formal settings. Incorporated instead of brushed entirely aside or credited as electives, this base of experience lays the foundation from which the learning (degree) plan is constructed. Thus the individual, not the institution, is responsible for determining the course new learning will take as informed by prior learning. From the outset, learners are empowered to make those decisions critical to their own academic growth. It is they who compose program curricula, devise the most appropriate methods of demonstrating proficiency, and enlist interdisciplinary-trained faculty as resources rather than professorial authorities in strictly defined departments or fields.

Structurally, Union learners are given a great deal of latitude in both the smaller and larger affairs affecting their learning. In the doctoral program, for instance, the student functions as committee chair, appoints faculty and peer members, and sets pre- and graduation meeting agendas. One would be hard pressed to locate another institution where matters this important are entrusted to the student. In addition, the learner instead of the college proposes the timetable for degree completion and proceeds toward it at a pace comfortable for the learner. Operationally, many of the usual academic accoutrements are also shunned. Apart from required, residential seminars, students need not submit to compulsory class attendance but work primarily at home or in learning cohorts consisting of peers. Courses of study are not prescribed but negotiated between the adult student and the faculty advisor, allowing for the formation of personalized learning plans. Records of scholastic progress are maintained by the Graduate School Office, but as graduation draws near it falls to the student to compose a narrative transcript describing noteworthy academic accomplishments as well as other "course" completions.

Psychologically, students retain a large measure of independence and are not reticent about challenging institutional power structures or testing boundaries. In the Union paradigm, learners have say in or control virtually every component of their program, from the application stage through conferral of degrees. Given such autonomy, nearly none of the usual tension characterizing student-teacher relationships arises, nor does the anarchy many academic purists predict will occur when students are given the power to design individual learning plans. Freed from the cultural baggage that exists at most universities, learners come to feel, many for the first time, the exhilaration of what it means to be a truly empowered participant in the process of discovery. For their part, faculty relish their role as facilitators and guides, rather than purveyors of knowledge who lord disciplinary secrets over students. Both learners and faculty at the Union agree that the most enduring way to educate a person is by thoughtfully screening out most traditional academic practices because these conventions perpetuate power imbalances and interpersonal frictions that do little apart from impeding learning.

The unifying thread running through these postmodern experiments is their utter fearlessness in rejecting convention. As we have seen, tradition is a powerful animal in the academic world and defiance of it one of the oldest taboos. Nonetheless, wherever educators continue to pursue educational schemes that respect the individual student and his or her capacity to become active agents in learning (Vernon, Lo Parco, and Marsick, 1993), programs like those mentioned earlier will still light the way.

POSTMODERN POSSIBILITIES FOR EMBRACING ADULTS AS STUDENTS

In this section, the aggregate work of Henry Giroux (1988a, 1988b, 1990, 1992) as well as William Tierney (1989, 1991, 1993) guide the discussion. These two educators have demonstrated both an abstract comprehension of and compassionate concern for the ultimate humanity of marginalized students that, in tandem, provide a beautifully balanced perspective for analysis.

Postmodernism addresses the prominent issues in adult education from a radically redefined perspective. Interestingly, all Knowles' andragogical principles have theoretical correspondents in the postmodern infrastructure. Through investigations of border andragogy, teachers and students as border crossers, and praxis as the ideal outcome of education, the reader will develop an informed understanding of the nature of postmodern education.

Even more important, these issues interplay to illustrate the present precarious state of affairs in adult educational programs. If I use border pedagogy to propose a better future, what am I saying about the current state of adult education? Throughout this and preceding chapters, it has been stressed that adult students are relegated to the status of Otherness, a culturally expendable role reserved for those "different" from the dominant majority. Giroux expands on this point:

At the same time it is important to understand how the experience of marginality at the level of everyday life lends itself to forms of oppositional and transformative consciousness. This is an understanding based on the need for those designated as Others to both reclaim and remake their histories, voices and visions part of a wider struggle. (1988b, p. 174)

Adult students are seen very differently across college campuses. Those institutions where ambivalence lingers over their presence stand to profit the most from the forthcoming discussion.

From Border Pedagogy to Border Andragogy

At its core, postmodern theory endorses critical resistance to the official teachings of established disciplines (Ahmed, 1992). While it does not summarily deny their educative potential, it posits that previously censured explanations, stories, and memories would embellish and therefore deepen the foundations of modernist science. Therefore, border pedagogy takes on the twofold task of not only creating new and alternative bodies of knowledge but examining how hegemony is rooted in primary institutional and pedagogical structures (Giroux, 1992). An instructional model that affirms and embraces these alternative interpretations warrants closer inspection in today's multicultural learning environments.

Postmodern theory extends the conceptual frontiers of a teaching methodology that commences with the intention of engaging adults and other marginal student groups. For critical and postmodern theorists, it is unthinkable to philosophize about pedagogy without taking into account the broader cultural considerations in which learning activities occur. Notions of cultural space, language, and epistemology (modes of knowing) are central to theorizing a border pedagogy (Giroux, 1988a). Further, it offers the opportunity for students collectively to meet and critique the multiple references that constitute different cultural codes and customs which may be foreign to the subculture they inhabit.

The term *border* is rich in allegory and meaning. It alludes not only to physical borders, but cultural borders historically created and socially reinforced that foster specific identities, behaviors, cultures, and social arrangements. Rosaldo (1989, p. 208), describing the spaces *within* these borders, elaborates:

More often than we usually care to think, our everyday lives are crisscrossed by border zones, pockets, and eruptions of all kinds. Social borders frequently become salient around such lines as sexual orientation, gender, class, race, ethnicity, nationality, age. . . . Such borderlands should be regarded not as analytically empty transitional zones, but as sites of creative cultural production that require investigation.

As these boundaries are generated by differences in social status and power, and are legitimated by dominant interests, they are extremely resilient. By reproducing the ruling culture, schools maintain their primacy as authoritative sources of knowledge. In turn, teachers naturally emerge as gatekeepers of the truth.

For adults, frames of reference from which to derive meaning are plentiful as they have been accumulated over the lifespan. Personal experience also provides a cognitive context against which knowledge and learning can be critically evaluated for their consistency in life situations. Yet there is more to border pedagogy than remapping the territory of science and teacher-pupil interactions along less paternalistic lines. As well as advocating a questioning of universal texts and master narratives, postmodernism stresses the agency of examining the "lived cultures" (Giroux, 1988a, p. 141) of students. By validating the cultural conditions that shape one's life, it encourages an expanded perceptual awareness and subsequently fosters a climate where real and authentic learning can occur.

After these conditions have been met, we may begin to talk about a new approach to reaching adults in terms of a border andragogy. Border anadragogy encourages the formulation and testing of new, unfamiliar ways of knowing (Lincoln, 1991, p. 25). In standard paradigms, students are exposed to the discipline's rules for knowledge acquisition. That is to say, they are taught that the search for solutions to problems in history or biology courses must follow a particular method endorsed by the discipline. Adults, having the benefit of real-world trial, often apply alternative modes of apprehending knowledge that frequently skirt or supersede disciplinary parameters. Because of this difference from younger students, postmodern educators should plan learning interventions where adults have the opportunity to flex, strengthen, and modify their own specialized ways of knowing.

Adult Students and Teachers as Border Crossers

Within the discourse of border andragogy, teachers and students must engage knowledge as border crossers (Hicks, 1988), persons traversing between worlds constructed along nexuses of power and plurality. For their part, adult students must be willing to cross over into realms of meaning, legends of knowledge, social relations, and belief systems that are constantly being negotiated and reterritorialized (Giroux, 1992) as new learning meets up with prior experiences and standing values.

Unlike pedagogy where the student is benignly deferent to an all-knowing teacher embodying a particular subject, postmodern educational theory repudiates this model as arcane, pedantic, and detrimental to learning. For learning to occur, the interaction between student and teacher must be dialogic. Didacticism is dead in postmodernity. In our time, learners and teachers are co-inquirers on the path to discovery. Vertical teacher-student relationships give way to leveled learning interactions. The conditions necessary to foster optimal conditions for a learning dialogue include (Giddens, 1979, p. 47): (1) agreement arrived at through rational debate; (2) complete and mutual understanding on the part of each participant in the discussion; and, most important, (3) an assertion of the "authentic right of the other to take part in the dialogue as an *autonomous and equal partner* [italics added]."

As transformative intellectuals, teachers must strive to help adult students comprehend the dominant value system, and to struggle to break down and overcome those ideological and cultural artifacts that prevent their empowerment (Giroux, 1988b). Such crucial work demands adult educators display a critical awareness of academic culture and what it treats as knowledge, and that they nurture this same ability in students. Yet there is something even more advantageous in this process. "By being able to listen critically to the voices of their students, teachers also become border crossers through their ability to make different narratives available to themselves and to legitimate difference as a basic condition for understanding the limits of one's own knowledge." (Giroux, 1992, p. 35). Thus we see how teachers as well as students will be exposed to new readings of knowledge and be afforded the opportunity to revisit their own conceptions of disciplinary borders. Tierney (1991) describes it as a collaborative effort wherein students and teacher unite to "avoid an ideological hegemony, where only one definition of reality is allowed to exist . . . so that the status quo is not maintained" (p. 43).

The concept of coming to terms with knowledge while at the same time grappling with cultural differences also requires a reassessment of the traditional view of faculty as authority figures. Here the work of Tierney (1989, p. 135) is highly illuminating. Teachers are regarded as authorities because they have certain knowledge. Knowledge, then, is perceived as a fixed, graspable body that some people possess (teachers) and others do not (students). In such a scenario, students cannot participate in the learning process on an equal footing. Adults are specifically hurt by this scheme because it dismisses their experiences as unsuitable for formal inquiry and thus reduces any influence they have in decision making over curricular content or instructional technique.

In border andragogy, however, the rules of engagement are significantly modified. Perhaps for the first time, an adult student feels the pleasure of being recognized for having a store of personal knowledge that complements and enriches subject matter presented in class discussions. Bagnall (1995) argues that this affirmation leads to the development of new perceptual frameworks informed by "the experience of past actions and the anticipation of future ones" (p. 84). In border andragogy, experience is credited, stories are recounted, and the lessons learned over the course of the adult's life are valued as integral to transformative learning.

Praxis and Action Learning

If, as critical theorists and postmodernists claim, transformation is the ultimate objective of education, how do we attain such an intangible outcome through our learning programs? What information, theoretical or practical, is available that might point us in the right direction?

The term *praxis*, in an educational context, first appeared in the writings of Brazilian educator Paulo Freire (1972a, 1972b, 1973). He used the term to describe the reflective process that accompanies genuine learning. Reflection upon learning should precipitate action on the part of the student who has been sufficiently enlightened so that failure to act would render the knowledge newly acquired inert. Freire initially employed *praxis* to describe his work with working-class adult students and his success in boosting literacy rates among them. It seems, as one might anticipate, that with their improved reading abilities, these workers consumed extensive political and economic writings awakening them to the need for solidarity and representation against unscrupulous imperialists and owners of capital.

Though these events are noteworthy, our attention must stay fixed on the principles of praxis, or action learning. Williams (1992, p. 39), citing Branstadter (1984), explains it more fully:

Action learning can be defined as the process of combining an abstract mental construct (usually moral, philosophical, or political reasoning) with a physical action that often lies outside social, economic, and political norms of behavior, both to test the validity of the construct and to reconstitute the social rules related to it.

Thus the strength of action learning lay in its translation of theory into practice, idea into act, a shortcoming all too frequent in most theorizing. Holford (1995) explains how action learning or "cognitive praxis" bridges the gap: "What rarely emerges at the level of theory is . . . that people themselves may contribute to the shaping of social knowledge in important ways" (p. 101). In such a scheme, students become creators of knowledge through action and appraisal, not just receptacles for it. Testing what is learned in class through an "alternating process of investigation and exploration" (Brookfield, 1985, p. 16) and then being inspired to act upon that knowledge in social encounters is something rarely advocated in institutionally based educational programs.

Heaney (1992, p. 55) underscores this very idea in stating that "learning cannot be separated from doing" and points to the pioneering work undertaken by Highlander Folk School, an educational institution founded by Myles Horton in the Tennessee foothills more than sixty years ago. Highlander, as an expressly different vehicle for the education of adults, had as its philosophical heart the notion that learning must be reified—brought to life—through active participation in movements and struggles happening in the world outside the campus. In Highlander thinking, there can be no substitute for direct and collective experiential learning. Not surprisingly, Highlander faculty and students figured prominently in the early civil rights and labor union movements that swept through the South in the 1960s. In consequence, its emphasis on social action provoked the ire of many enemies whose power and privileges were threatened by the forces of progress and who worked to see it closed. In this trailblazing role, Highlander successfully spanned the usual rift dividing theory and practice in adult learning and survived as a prototype for postmodern education. Lauding the ground that was broken, Heaney (1992, p. 56) rebukes mainstream adult educators and traditional programs for continuing to march blindly in step to a "comparatively monotonous drummer," noting that "Highlander, as a prophet and critic, is more easily honored from an academic distance than emulated in practice."

With the concept of praxis and the practice of action learning, the adult student develops new reasoning skills and companion behaviors that contextualize knowledge. Herein enters the postmodern notion of "counter-memory" (Kaplan, 1987) as a precondition for action learning by broadening the perceptual lens that adults use to examine and critique new learning. Counter-memory implies a "critical reading of how the past informs the present and how the present reads the past" (Aronowitz and Giroux, 1991, p. 124). Thus knowledge newly acquired is contextualized when the adult student connects it to and compares it against past remembrances of lasting cognitive impact.

SUMMARY

The preceding discussion should allow the reader to see the potential of postmodernism in conceptualizing adult education. In spite of its darker diagnosis of the current social decline, any downward spiral can still be offset by thoughtful action. Rather than allow ourselves to split into communities segregated along racial, economic, or cultural lines, we have the power to alter our future. Reclaiming the discourses and dreams of the Other is a pivotal first step. Resisting the momentum to engage ascendant groups and their representations of reality is immoral. After all, it is in the blurring of tradition with novelty, science with feeling, and scholarship with folklore that a fuller account of humanity emerges and does justice to people in their infinite variety.

Michael Awkward, an African-American literary theorist, celebrates this commingling of cultures as essential to academic evolution. He asserts that only through the articulation and critiquing of subordinate tellings and alternative renditions can academia make amends for the sin of centuries of orthodoxy to the canon. Even the most erudite elements in the ivory tower have something to gain. For, as we have seen, neither students nor faculty live in a social vacuum, and the academic milieu can only be enhanced by this broadening of views.

We are all, to some degree, formed by the cultural criss-crossings of race, gender, class, sexuality, and religion that serve, I believe, to determine much of the nature of our lives in a contemporary American "meeting ground" characterized by unprecedented access to the images, perspectives, and behaviors of locational Others. (Awkward, 1995, p. 14)

Though some display an aversion to the idea, adult students and those that teach them would be enriched by the admission of individual experiences into a class setting that previously prohibited all but disciplinary versions of knowledge. Gergen (1991, p. 173) has described this expansion of perception in colorful but essentially accurate terms, contending that in the postmodern age, we are "becoming increasingly populated with fragments of the other." Intrinsically, this phenomenon is good since each "fragment we incorporate from others is also an acquisition of value," a "small voice" of Otherness taking up residence in us, honorably retelling the struggles it encountered along the way.

Chapter 6

Critical Postmodern Leadership for Adult Education

> People frequently ask us, "Are leaders born or made?" No one
> knows for sure. . . . We can, however, tell you this for certain: every
> exceptional leader we know is also a learner.
> —J. Kouzes and B. Posner, *The Leadership*
> *Challenge* (1987)

This chapter presents an alternative view of leadership for adult education as well as a humanistic philosophical position for its leaders.
Academic practices and "truths" generated in bygone eras have apparently fallen short in addressing the educational, social, and cultural
needs of today's older learner. Earlier chapters in this book have gone
to great lengths in chronicling the nature and scope of those anachro-
nistic, biased and contradictory tendencies contained in and impinging
upon the art of adult education. What emerged was a theoretically
supportable consensus that change must occur, that what passed as
acceptable leadership in adult programs until now simply perpetuated
ways of marginalizing nontraditional students.

If, as Ilsey (1992, p. 30) declares, "adult educators are agents for
making the world a better place," how they lead programs serving this
population merits a hard look. It follows, then, that our emphasis
should be on synthesizing theory and practice into a new paradigm for
adult education leadership. Ideally, the model we propose will rely
heavily on emancipatory insights gleaned from critical and postmodern
theory. More than that, however, it should be grounded enough in
practice so the reader can co-construct a fresh approach to adult
education along with the author, one valuing the difference and

occasional dissent older students bring to the academy. If a bias has existed in traditional higher education against nontraditional students, which the evidence amassed in this work seems to suggest, it is incumbent upon deans and directors of adult learning to challenge former beliefs and behaviors. Ilsey concurs, noting that our attention in "adult education, until recently, ignored groups of people who were countercultural or resisted the status quo" (p. 30). The coming generation of educational leaders this essay presages should diligently work to change all that.

The first half of this discussion is an introduction to critical postmodern theory and the exposition of a leadership philosophy derived from it. Given its conceptual thrust, the text will supply an overview of critical postmodernism's origins and breadth to acquaint the reader with its potential uses. Dwelling less on abstraction, the second half of the essay will demonstrate how the proposed philosophy might find practical application to issues faced by adult education administrators and faculty. The opening section includes a historical synopsis and a statement of philosophical position. The second, or applied, section covers issues such as transformative leadership, power, conflict, and community in academic surroundings.

It may seem as though this analysis takes a turn early on toward the philosophical and never quite returns to the concrete. Throughout this book, I have tried to anchor all theoretical musings in reality (a fundamental theme in adult learning as proposed by Malcolm Knowles), employing many examples from the literature, from stories of adult students, and from my own career experience to highlight areas that might otherwise seem too remote in the obscure realm of abstraction. I will make the same effort here. However, the subject of leadership does not lend itself particularly well to functional breakdown and analysis.

This inclination is natural in the study of leadership. Inspirational texts, political memoirs, self-help seminars, and TQM/CQI corporate workshops abound, all claiming to impart the latest vision of leadership to sundry audiences. Each boasts that it can bridge the gap between thought and action, transmute idea into impulse. Whether they actually accomplish these claims is, predictably, in the eye of the beholder. Although I would like to assure adult students and those who sponsor programs for them that something more profound and pragmatic will transpire as a result of their reading the folowing discussion, I cannot be certain of this. Once again, it will depend largely on the mind-set of the reader in its openness to innovation.

For beleaguered administrators, program managers, and department chairs preoccupied with the immediacy of educating adults, this emphasis may be insufficient. Therefore, I will also spend time on practical matters in this examination. After all, adult education leaders cannot eschew utilitarian concerns. British andragogist Michael Collins (1991, p. 1) describes the material, not just philosophical, "crisis" confronting those of us in the field:

We can refer initially to the difficulties adult educators have always come up against in maintaining a firm, minimally financed, institutional basis from which to practise their vocation. The struggle for a share of resources and legitimation is much more clear-cut for adult education components operating within larger institutional settings. (In this regard, one has only to consider, for example, the marginalized situation of university extension divisions.)

Marginalization—those who have read the preceding chapters are very familiar with, perhaps even weary of, this term and its connection to the adult student experience in traditional higher education. However, I suggest that it is the risk of marginalization that necessitates the articulation of a nascent view of leadership for the field. Until now, the popular impression of adult programs within academia, as shown throughout this book, is that they are inferior (Hart, 1990; Tisdell, 1993b; Welton, 1993). Consequently those invested with the leadership of adult interventions should have an acute interest in any dialogue that strays from the tedious repertoire of topics commonly presented in refereed journals and scholarly symposia.

THEORETICAL TIME AND CONTEMPORARY VISTAS

The once heralded golden age of human history—modernity, an era that spanned from the eighteenth-century Enlightenment through the first half of this century (Fox, 1995)—can now be critically appraised for the destructive tendencies it harbored. The legacy of modernity has become ever clearer: disintegration of families, the cheapening of human life, a balkanization of social relations, and an ecological pillaging of the planet (Spretnak, 1988). Where we once were joined by kinship and cosmology, modernism forced us to forsake all that was sacred in our ancient traditions and beliefs. Our connectedness to the earth, each other, and a creator were brusquely swept aside in the march of progress. The pursuit of science and technology became a new world religion, and those people and cultures who followed premodern social and spiritual values were disdainfully branded "third world."

After several catastrophic transnational events rocked the Western social order to its foundations—two world wars and horribly costly experiments in communism and fascism—the modern epoch crashed to a close. Reason, Truth, and Science as cornerstones of modern industrial society were exposed for the contradiction and barbarism they contained in advancing the imperialism of European "civilization" (Giroux, 1988b). A subtle aversion to modern life slowly crept over people. Those who survived the disasters were left with a vacant, numbing feeling that gradually permeated literature, art, architecture and other forms of "postmodern" expression. Robert Wright (1995, p. 50) captures both the growing disenchantment with modern techno-society and the psychological void it leaves behind in painting this colloquial scene:

VCR's and microwaves have their virtues, but in the everyday course of our highly efficient lives, there are times when something seems deeply amiss. Whether burdened by an overwhelming flurry of daily commitments or stifled by a sense of social isolation (or oddly, both); whether mired for hours in a sense of life's pointlessness or beset for days by unresolved anxiety; whether deprived by long work-weeks from quality time with offspring . . . whatever the source of stress, we at times get the feeling that modern life isn't what we were designed for.

While the ruins of modernity still smoldered, the light of a new day was dawning—the postmodern. As such things are reckoned, this era began unnoticed in the years following World War II (Matthews and Noorgard, 1984) but did not gather momentum or catch sociologists' interest as a nameable phenomenon until relatively recently. Learning its lessons from history, postmodernism spurned the teachings and ideology of modernity as pompously incomplete and criminally unful-filling, citing numerous and chronic social problems: drugs, crime, poverty, despair—how modernism failed us.

In addition, postmodern theory revolved around the long-term social impact of marginalization. Groups excluded from public life, those whose discourses were categorically muted in national, regional, and local politics, were at last recognized and their tellings affirmed as integral to our collective consciousness (Falk, 1988). The aggregate work of critical and postmodern theorists helped the socially sensible see the many paradoxes and injustices that had been embedded in social relations. Their analyses illustrated the persistence of oppression at institutional and interpersonal levels. They spoke to the conflict between what is and ought to be in the social and economic order of things. They focused on the issue of *difference* as *the* single defining reality (Quinnan, 1995b) of American and academic culture. Unfortunately, they also stopped short of providing us with much more than a list of the problems. Where might we begin our search for solutions?

Critical postmodernism opens one theoretical avenue in rendering a reply. It uses the best of both critical and postmodern theories in constructing a worldview uniquely its own (Aronowitz and Giroux, 1991). Affirming that current social structures are tainted by oppression (critical theory) and that the source of hegemony lies largely with a refusal to acknowledge cultures outside the dominant (postmodernism), critical postmodernism rises from a solid foundation. For its part, it reclaims the traditions of the past and revivifies them in the here and now. Critical postmodernism avers that in premodern times things of value did indeed exist, such as communality, responsibility, and an expectation for meaningful social intercourse. Additionally, it disdains modernism's antisocial preoccupation with the individual (Jarvis, 1992), ponders the implication of postmodernism's extreme plurality, and asserts that society and its harmonious continuation are concerns superseding personal gratification.

Herein rests the uniqueness of the critical postmodern project; it is both constructive and revisionary (Griffin, 1988). Unlike critical theory and postmodernism, it stresses a rebirthing of social covenants and institutions, rather than contenting itself with their dismantling and razing. The tenor of the dialectic changes from interrogation of an object/subject for its self-annulling properties to a second genesis. The reformulation of an adult education enterprise premised on the richness of such a theory provides the perfect laboratory for testing these hypotheses.

Finally, it is important to note that "critical postmodernism" does not belong to a particular place or period in time. Unlike modernity and postmodernity, which have comparatively visible chronological borders, one cannot discern critical postmodern philosophy, religion, or leadership tied to a discrete place in history. Of all three theories, critical postmodernism is the most disinclined to be fixed in the continuum of time. Many of its ideas as presented here evolved during the zenith of modernism, coming from thinkers such as Martin Luther King or Mahatma Gandhi, who were disillusioned with the way human affairs seemed headed. Other of its primary assumptions coalesced in the postmodern critique, a true *world*view which conjectures the prospect of a society free from prejudice against its "Other" members (Rosaldo, 1989).

At issue, then, is the expounding of a theory of leadership that treats and reconstructs propositions from former and current schools of educational thought. If this lends an eclectic flavor to our project, we graciously accept it. For it is only from a historically informed language of critique that we encounter new possibilities for human freedom and happiness (Aronowitz and Giroux, 1985).

A Critical Postmodern Philosophy

If our wish is to offer a new strategy for leading in adult education, we must cast aside antiquated notions of governance and decision making born during the modern epoch. Little inspiration can be derived from the Newtonian schematic—organizations as machines and their leaders as technicians—that still dominates the science of organizational structure and behavior. To shake off these vestiges and stimulate a contemporary discussion, *metanoia* is required. This term was used by Peter Senge in *The Fifth Discipline* (1990) to describe a process of cognitive change. In addition to its Greek etymology, Senge interprets it as a "shift of the mind" and "the most accurate word in Western culture to describe what happens in a learning organization" (p. 13). Senge contends that the reason so many organizations suffer from mediocrity is their leadership's inability to divorce themselves from thinking that precludes growth, experimentation, and learning.

The critical postmodern educator must entertain a similar "shift of the mind" away from standard models of academic leadership. Senge suggests that the next generation of academic and corporate leaders will lead from a "systems paradigm" rather than cling to intransigent, mechanistic views of institutions. They will know that the culture of any human institution should not be likened to a machine or its leadership reduced to an organizational chart, but rather to the body— organic, with each part essential to the overall health of the organism. "Systems thinking is a discipline for seeing wholes. It is a framework for seeing interrelationships rather than things, for seeing patterns of change rather than 'static snapshots'" (p. 68). Educationally, this implies a recognition that various cells are needed to maintain stasis in the body of the academic community. One such cell group, adult learners, cannot be cut off or quarantined from the larger body without the entire campus suffering for it.

To provide a wider explanation of critical postmodern education, we must begin by exploring the conceptual and practical mortar shoring up its foundations. Once its salient concepts are understood, we can begin to narrow our focus in navigating the theoretical terrain it maps. Supreme among them is the notion of "similarity within difference" (Kanpol, 1992), a summons to academic community that is welcoming of cultural difference.

In *Building Communities of Difference,* Tierney (1993) discussed critical postmodern educational practice in an emotionally appealing but intellectually piecemeal fashion. He did not present this theory in any coherent or logical fashion, but pulled together assorted bits of philosophy and wisdom in molding his own "cultural politics of hope" (p. 22). Apart from its intriguing overtones, this phrase hints at several crucial aspects of critical postmodernism. First, it denotes a respect for the cultural constitution of the student, teacher, and others involved in learning. Second, the phrase acknowledges the indissoluble link between cultural and political status, as well as how the former determines the latter in institutional settings. Last, it titillates with a glimmer of hope for a future yet to be shaped, reminding us that together we have the power to influence its course.

Another fundamental premise in critical postmodernism is community and the necessity of its establishment despite wide differences among campus constituencies (Richardson, 1991; Pittman, 1994). While we discuss community at length later on, it must be introduced here as a salient component in the critical postmodern vision being endorsed for adult education. Because of an inescapable interdependence among participants, much greater than what occurs in society at large, intellectual "community" must be sought after at all costs. The view of community espoused by critical postmodernism, however idyllic, is not blinded by naive notions of blissful harmony. Instead, we are sophisticated enough in theory to know that pluralistic communities exist in a sort of controlled tension and the push for consensus between persons is "managed hegemony" (Freiberg, 1979, p. 16). Critical postmodern communities allow for widely dispersed cultural, economic, and social positions and attempt to accord them equal weight in maintaining group integrity. Dissent is not feared or rooted out, but actively encouraged with the express hope that dialogue is the primary democratic and transformational event in communal life. Differences, no matter how insurmountable they may seem at first, can ultimately be negotiated through a larger concern for justice and autonomy.

To reify—make tangible—critical postmodern theory into practices adult education leaders might use, our plans and programs must be based in a set of shared moral principles. Support for this mooring in a collective ethics appears throughout research and in multiple disciplines. In *Prospects for a Common Morality* (1993) Outka and Reeder enlist ethicists, philosophers, clergy, and sociologists to consider this precise question, inquiring whether "the notion of common morality is an illusion" (p. 4). Their conclusions are mixed. Alan Donagan (1993) speaks for many of the scholars in commenting that, while the possibility of all cultures adopting the same moral code is nil, the spirit underlying whatever ethics they do espouse will become more alike. However, assorted viewpoints are expressed. Adams (1993, p. 107) supplies a different perspective: "The moral agreement democracy needs, however, is not to be found in a common ethical theory or even a common theory of justice, but in the unsystematic plurality of agreements that constitute common morality." Out of chaos, order may arise, and while we may war over larger matters, a common ethics begins with working out agreement on the smallest issues. Once a level of trust develops, the academic community has a moral platform upon which it can build and reorganize.

The lifework of Robert Greenleaf sheds further light on the ethical imperative for leadership. Author of the seminal treatise *The Servant as Leader* (1970, revised 1991) and several related essays (1972, 1979) addressing the moral dimensions of leadership predicated on service to others, or *primus inter pares* (first among equals), he provides a magnificent glimpse of critical postmodern philosophy in leadership. Unfortunately, Greenleaf's writings can be explored here only briefly, for their depth is the substance of voluminous study. I recognize that I am doing him and my reader a disservice by merely touching the surface of his "servant leadership" philosophy, but encourge readers to explore his writings more deeply for themselves.

After a medley of career experiences—in corporate human resources, as a college professor, and as a consultant to government—Greenleaf settled into an active retirement and therein made his greatest contributions. In this retrospective phase of his life, he began to refine his ideas and began writing about his unique vision of leadership. Early in his first essay we become acquainted with his purposes:

I am hopeful for these times, despite the tension and conflict, because . . . a fresh critical look is being taken at the issues of power and authority, and people are beginning to learn, however haltingly, to relate to one another in less coercive and more creatively supporting ways. A new moral principle is emerging which holds that the only authority deserving one's allegiance is that which is freely and knowingly granted by those led to the leader in response to and in proportion to, the clearly evident servant stature of the leader. (1991, p. 4)

What then, does his reasoning portend for leadership style? How does the servant-leader define and comport her/himself? On these important issues, Greenleaf is straightforward. "The servant-leader *is* servant first. . . . It begins with the natural feeling that one wants to serve, to serve *first*. Then conscious choice brings one to aspire to lead" (p. 7). In this sense, s/he stands apart from the type of leader in it for personal power or material gain.

The difference manifests itself in the care taken by the servant first to make sure that other people's highest priority needs are being served. The best test, and difficult to administer, is: do those served grow as persons: do they, *while being served*, become healthier, wiser, freer, more autonomous, more likely themselves to become servants. *And*, what is the effect on the least privileged in society: will he benefit, or, at least, will he not be further deprived.

His message is immersed in humanism and hope. In addition to a concern for social justice, the servant leader is energized by another calling. "The interest in and affection for his followers" that a leader shows is a "mark of true greatness " (p. 13) and admits leaders to the select company of history's preeminent figures, from Christ to Martin Luther King (1958), who displayed a similar selfless compassion for their followers.

Suffused in the work of Greenleaf and others is the theme of unconditional love. In spite of myriad differences, young or old, black or white, poor or wealthy, each of us believes in the necessity of finding a joint space where these differences can be talked about and understood. As marvelous creations in ourselves, surely we can recognize the miraculous in Others.

TRANSFORMATION AND POWER

Transformational Learning

Instead of taking on the gargantuan task of defining leadership, a topic that has exhausted the intellectual reserves of countless academic, political, and corporate notables, I will proceed from a different strategy and will outline the discussion with an alternative framework. In this instance, the perspective used rises from theory. I will draw a composite image of a new academic leader interpolating ideas and insights from critical and postmodern theory. Heaney (1993, p. 14) gives us a glimpse of what theoretically informed education can do: "Adult education can, like the reading of texts, provoke reflection and critical judgement as a prelude to change.

Foremost is the concept of adult educators as agents of change, or transformation (Clark, 1993), in the fullest sense of the term. After investigating the underpinnings of this new leadership project, I will discuss qualities that adult educators should embody to effect lasting change in an institution stubbornly resistant to it (O'Toole, 1995). In addition, adult educators must remain cognizant of the political repercussions of innovation. As intellectuals, legitimators, and enactors of ideas and social practices, we carry out a "function that is eminently political in nature" (Aronowitz and Giroux, 1985, p. 31).

To bring about transformation, the educator of adults must understand and promote "learning as a change of consciousness" (Clark, 1993, p. 53). If education is to be the liberating force it proclaims to be, it must make an indelible impression on those actively involved in its multiform processes. Until now, education of the variety usually seen in American colleges and universities has been largely preoccupied with reinforcing the dominant social structure and relations of power. The curriculum, teaching methods, and academic culture have effectively conspired to perpetuate the existing political and economic order. Transformational learning challenges all that. As its explicit mission, it seeks to reshape "people; they are different afterward, in ways both they and others can recognize" (p. 47). When applied to adult learning, it permits the student and teacher finally to encounter knowledge in the broader cultural context that influenced its construction. Permanently impacting the adult student is a grand but somewhat evasive aim. Can higher education actually attain this noble goal? If so, where might the critical postmodern educator begin?

Empowerment is a concept much discussed in critical theory and radical educational circles. Later it was extrapolated into the debate concerning multiculturalism that came to dominate much of the current dialogue in higher education. Most recently it has even been purloined by agents of the status quo—accrediting agencies—in how they charge member institutions to conceptualize campus diversity (ACSCU-WASC, 1994). Through overuse the term lost much of its original luster as its meaning has been diluted by whatever group, conservative or liberal, employs it for its own purposes. However, empowering adults and those who work with them in academic settings has been and still is a fundamental mission in the radical movement, traceable to the groundbreaking work of Paulo Freire (1972a, 1972b). Unlike the opportunists, this camp has never vacillated in its commitment to equality by reexamining the political, social, and cultural ramifications of formal education. Ironically, it seems to have taken the educational establishment almost twenty-five years to enter into the discussion on these dimensions of learning—and suddenly with a vengeance. Today one would be hard-pressed to attend an academic symposium or professional association meeting where the term "empowerment" does *not* resound through the corridors.

Simply put, empowerment may be understood as the "ability to think and act critically" (Giroux, 1992, p. 11) by coming to grips with the historical forces defining each person's and each group's current existence. To bring about the lasting change promised by transformation theorists, however, we need elaboration. William Tierney (1991, p. 8) responds:

Empowerment is a complex process that takes place within a matrix of specific cultural relations . . . empowerment is a process whereby individuals come to self-understandings of their place in society. Empowered individuals are able to see how the larger society has formed, shaped, and mangled their own lives and interpreted realities. These same individuals are then able to re-form and reshape their lives and those of their families and friends.

Although this descriptions hints at the efficacy of collective discovery as the road to empowerment, any awakening must start with the individual. Heightened group consciousness develops afterward. Tierney informs us that teachers or institutions cannot wave a magic wand and transform students merely by wishing it or using fiery rhetoric. Academia can, however, "generate the conditions for empowerment, but ultimately, those who are dispossessed and voiceless take control of their own lives" (p. 8).

Rethinking the Nature of Power

Power often determines status in hierarchically ordered, patriarchical societies like ours (Kuh, 1990). This pattern is reflected and repeated throughout the social structures of capitalism (Agger, 1989), where the holders of capital enjoy privilege and authority that the laboring masses do not. Hence our economic system and the class divisions it engenders are replicated across social institutions—government, church, and schools—all of whom adopted organizational schemes consistent with this general pattern (Chin and Benne, 1985; Wheatley, 1992).

By the end of the 1800s, colleges and universities displayed systems of governance that could accurately be considered authoritarian. Any graduate students in American higher education is familiar with names like Eliot (Harvard), Angell (Michigan), and White (Cornell), presidents—and autocrats (Veysey, 1965)—of three prestigious institutions. Moving forward from the turn of the century, power eventually became diffused throughout policymaking entities (faculty senates/committees) and less concentrated in the office of the president. Nonetheless, leadership remained an oligarchy, or rule of the few—presidents, deans, and department chairs. Obviously, then, power was still the academic leader's greatest asset—power to hire and tenure faculty, secure fiscal resources, or determine curricular content with little interference from inside or without. Even now, many institutions continue to operate upon vertically based governance models.

Fortunately, critical postmodernism conceives of power in an utterly different fashion. Here power is not ascribed simply by place in the pecking order, nor is it imparted by proxy of the organization. In traditional leadership schemes, authority is foundational, inherited by whomever occupies a particular role in the chain of command. In contrast, critical postmodernism views power as generative (O'Toole, 1995). The term *generative* implies that power, for lack of a better term, is a growing, living dynamic initiated by the leader but shared among those supporters who willingly consent to be led and so entrust the leader to act in stewardship for the larger collective.

In this unique way, power becomes relational instead of prescribed. The new leader knows that relationships take precedence over one's title and the authority it imputes. As a result, a leader strives to create a discipleship who share the vision and want to exert an impact in their own domains to help attain that vision. Plain and simple, this new kind of leader empowers followers, nurturing strong subordinates into "potential successors" (O'Toole, 1995, p. 53) and clears a path for them to achieve instead of keeping them tightly leashed. Power, then, does not unilaterally favor the leader but becomes dispersed and in flux, always in negotiation (Foucault, 1980) with the ebb and flow of relations between the leader and his constituency.

CRITICAL POSTMODERN LEADERSHIP—A PROFILE

A recipe for making the perfect adult education dean, department chair, or program administrator is nowhere to be found. Any effort to claim otherwise should be regarded skeptically. The qualities and character necessary for leadership are far too elusive to pin down in a formula or deduce through analysis. Yet we seem comfortable enough uttering certain maxims about leading. We seldom hesitate to express what traits the "good" leader should naturally possess. Trying to isolate the difference between leading and managing, Bennis (1989, p. 18) supplies a representative tidbit: "Leaders are people who do the right thing; managers are people who do things right."

From the fuzziness that such statements evoke, we can sense the vague but awesome burden placed upon academic leaders. We expect them to display an amazing array of talents (Kouzes and Posner, 1987). They should invariably act from a moral center, inspire trust among students and colleagues, be adept financial administrators, speak well, listen even better, and dazzle us with a vision for those institutions and programs they lead. This may be too tall an order in the present reality.

Expectations for leaders in adult education are even more demanding. In the 1992 publication he edited, *Rethinking Leadership in Adult and Continuing Education*, Paul Edelson (p. 13) asks a loaded question to those who would lead in adult learning: "Despite the opportunities within adult and continuing education, there is evidence that some deans and directors, even when successful, are unwilling to remain in the field. . . . Does the much discussed marginality of adult and continuing education promote this outward mobility?" He argues that political leadership has become an indisputable "fact of life" for adult educators, who must accept it or face extinction. For Edelson, longevity in the profession is contingent upon adult educators' astuteness in the political realities of leading in academic organizations. He implores us to rise to our roles as "diplomats charged with representing this emerging 'state'" (p. 11) in the larger federation that is the university.

Assuming that they cultivate a measure of political acumen, adult educators must reflect on the place of leadership in their service area and what, given those parameters, would constitute an effective "leader." McGaughey (1992) concludes that this reflective process should culminate in the evolution of a persona she calls the "symbolic leader." Such persons take on the burden of creating and living a vision for the programs they steward, thus becoming the symbolic figure "who frames and reinforces the values and beliefs defining the culture of the . . . education unit" (p. 39). By way of support, Bensimon, Newmann, and Birnbaum (1989) add that symbolic leaders persuade others to reexamine institutional lore and the values it espouses. They then have the choice of either rededicating themselves to it or generating a new mythology. A parallel to the symbolic leader might be the village shaman in tribal societies, who served as visionary, interpreter of signs, leader of rituals, and mythmaker.

While McGaughey's work is instructive in extracting the role of metaphor in leadership, it neglects to explore fully the centrality of values. Thus inserting a critical theoretical perspective into the discussion at this juncture seems most appropriate. Cognizant that we are all products of socialization and socially formed by the dominant culture, we must logically concede that our "actions are never unbiased or value free" (Edelson, 1992, p. 8). The mind-sets we bring to leadership are similarly influenced by normative interests. Because of the plurality of positions among disparate individuals in contemporary times (D'Souza, 1991), lingering cultural biases in the educator could be particularly harmful to any emergent or unorthodox view of leadership. As new and unique cohorts of students are now entering college, adults prominent among them, academic leaders must be especially attuned to meeting different needs and expectations without tacitly or overtly imposing a leadership strategy that denigrates or excludes the needs of Other populations.

The new leader also exhibits professional concerns unlike those of his modernist counterpart. Where hierarchy once ruled in academic governance, leveling now reigns. If influence was a prized commodity in organizations, communication replaced it. Where simple courtesy used to suffice, interpersonal trust has become the mainstay for erecting a network of support and inspiring performance.

What distinguishes the new leader from the old is his or her focus on relationships instead of power. O'Toole (1995, p. 44) notes that "leaders respect people. Leadership is about relationships. Relationships count more than structure." Departing from conventional wisdom, leaders must recreate organizational structure away from the "tyranny of custom and ideology." People are paramount. Bureaucracy, policy, and procedure are secondary and should not determine the nature or quality of our relationships with students and colleagues in the organization.

Academically, the new leader can assume the role of an adult education professor, program coordinator, or college dean. Vocation within the academy does not preclude one from engaging in the work of the transformative intellectual. Too often, administrators are perceived only as bureaucrats or technicians charged with keeping the academic machinery running routinely (Bennis, 1976, 1984), while faculty assume the critical task of educating students. In fact, administrators also play a prominent role in shaping the wider campus milieu in which students and faculty interact. Deans and student service professionals must be seen as specialists who create and monitor the total campus environment (Delworth and Hanson, 1989), including learning experiences that occur outside the classroom. Further, the attitudes and behaviors they model go a long way in engendering support for academic and cocurricular learning initiatives. Leadership may be exercised in many domains, and administrators must realize that the work they do is every bit as important as classroom instruction.

WORKING TOWARD A CULTURAL POLITICS OF HOPE IN ADULT EDUCATION: LEADING THROUGH AGAPE

The politics of critical postmodernism require a thoughtful and sensitive reading (Griffin, 1988) in accounting for the legacies of its theoretical ancestors as well as depicting an entirely fresh vision for adult education. Critical theory championed issues of oppression, resistance, and conflict as endemic to colleges stratified along class lines. Assuming that unjust social and economic conditions continue to plague capitalist nations, critical scholars rally around the cause of disadvantaged groups in their struggle for equality. To this same conversation, postmodernism adds alternative interpretations of social history from the perspective of the excluded, a realignment of norms from center to subcultural axes, and a refocusing from class to cultural issues as the focus of its inquiries.

Where adult education meets critical theory is in its longing for academic acceptance and better treatment for its students, faculty, and administrators. This intersection finds richer description in the words of Aronowitz and Giroux (1985, p. 42):

We see educational theory as having a deep commitment to developing schools as sites that prepare students to participate in and struggle to develop democratic public life. This means that the value of educational theory and practice should be linked to providing the conditions for teachers and students to understand schools as public spheres dedicated to forms of self- and social empowerment.

By this the authors underscore the point that colleges and universities are forums for democratic engagement, a dress rehearsal for students, adult and youth, to obtain the fundamental civic skills required for active citizenship in a free society. If colleges claim to embody those virtues most cherished in our culture—truth, equality, and opportunity—they should especially be manifest in the programs created to serve nontraditional students. How seriously academic institutions and leaders take this responsibility varies considerably.

In today's postmodern world, issues of politics, culture, and education are hopelessly entangled (Giroux, 1988a). Educators cannot adequately treat one without addressing, willingly or not, the others. Since multiplicity in histories, aesthetics, and discourses are the defining characteristics of postmodern living, higher education has felt increasing pressure to democratize. Times have forced it to adopt, publicly at least, a more inclusive perspective on knowledge. Educational theorists have also shown teachers and administrators the firm correlation of knowledge to power (Foucault, 1973; Spring, 1988).

What leadership should aspire to, then, is what has been coined by Tierney (1993) as *cultural democracy*: "Cultural democracy involves the enactment of dialogue and action that are based on a framework of trying to understand and honor cultural difference, rather than of subjugating such difference to mere attributes of an individual's identity" (p. 11). The catalyst for creating a cultural democracy lay with an "ability to view one's life within forms of oppression, with the ultimate hope and possibility for both personal and social transformation" (Kanpol, 1992, p. 31). Logically, we must critically comprehend our origins and the circumstances that have forged our individual and social selves before we can decide where we want to go. Adult students, having had more years to experience struggle and challenge assumptions made by the dominant culture, are well prepared to participate in academic communities so organized.

Laclau and Mouffe (1985) spent significant time exploring the theoretical spaces necessary to foster cultural democracy and resolved that it entailed collective reflection on both struggle and possibility. They allude to this process as the *democratic imaginary*. In brief, the imaginary is contextualized—or made meaningful to participants— through investigating the set of struggles that highlight different forms of resistance in different places and times, but having common elements or moments. The example they provide is the shared experiences of feminist and civil rights movements. Properly undertaken, the democratic imaginary can unite disparate groups of students, particularly adults, within an ethos and "notion of solidarity" (Mouffe, 1988, p. 100).

The chief contribution of critical postmodern theorizing, concomitant with its realization of a democratic imaginary, distills down to its advocacy of "similarity within difference" (Kanpol, 1992, p. 115). This notion exhorts students, teachers, and campus officials to transcend their own "politics of positionality" (Awkward, 1995) that shades personal perspective and seek to establish a learning environment that credits difference and diversity of persons and experiences without according preference to any one of them.

Theorizing might be transformed into practice in the prime directive we choose to undergird our academic interventions. To be sure, there are many options. However, one essential principle around which adult education could revolve and serve as an inspiration for the university arises in *agape* (Outka, 1972). "Agape" is a classical Greek word denoting a particular type of love—the utterly selfless, benevolent regard one has for others much like the servant-leader's motivation alluded to earlier by Greenleaf (1991). It is an honest altruism, a love unhindered by conditions or qualifications. Tierney (1993, p. 23) observes that an academic "organization that works from the ideal of agape operates in a fundamentally different manner from other organizations. The underlying tenet here is that all life is interrelated. We are so connected that if you are in pain, so am I. In this light it is impossible to have a healthy institution when different individuals and constituencies are in pain."

Other scholars (e.g., Hesburgh, 1988; Yearley, 1993) suggest that formal educational programs that are ethically based prove to be the most enduring, if not in the length of their lifespan, then at least in the imprint they make at both individual and community levels. An adult educator similarly motivated by agape holds the key to the most ephemeral yet treasured of all academic dreams—formation of a true learning community.

Conflict

On today's multicultural campuses—which describes all but the most cloistered residential colleges—differences in opinions will vary widely and passionately. From such diversity, conflicts are certain to emerge. "Conflict, then, is a natural and expected outcome of this form of academic and social mixing, and one must be prepared to address conflict constructively if one is to realize the highest ideals of a multicultural democratic community" (Livingston and Berger, 1994, p. 428). As disagreement unfolds and contentious issues must be resolved, the question of justice arises. How institutions handle the discord coming from difference and, more important, deal with the protests of disadvantaged student groups, such as adults, reflect their authenticity in asserting democratic aims.

Postmodernism, unlike the managed tension sought in modernity's drive for consensus, anticipates conflict as a "natural" and dynamic process when opposing views are aired. However, postmodern theory ends with the public articulation and hearing of multiple, subordinate perspectives (Rorty, 1989). Such is the absolute limit of Otherness in this scheme.

Critical postmodern thought takes it one step beyond—toward mediation. We are not powerless and need not sit idly by as disparities proliferate to the point of becoming irreconcilable. Unhappy with merely pronouncing disagreement unavoidable, critical postmodernism explores the ways differences can be understood and offers suggestions for creating conditions allowing them to be bridged. Communicative action, originally a Habermasian construct, provides one possible avenue for negotiating among adversarial positions. Collins (1991, p. 12) expands on this:

Communicative action describes an ideal, though conceivably achievable, group learning experience where participants put forward their own views on the problem at hand, listen carefully and respectfully to those of others, and seriously examine all relevantly identified information introduced to the situation. It does not take the form of debate, or the mere weighing of pros and cons. The process is more rational and democratic—a kind of ongoing, thoughtful conversation.

One shortcoming in this prescription is its reliance on a rational and democratic dialogue. When oppressed people confront those who represent the ruling interests, cooler heads do not always prevail (Montero, 1995), especially as the dominant regime and the under-privileged usually have very dissimilar agendas. Critical postmodernism perceives the imbalance in power and objectives as a potential impediment to dialogue, and attacks the "myth of organizational rationality" (Morgan, 1986, p. 195) which says that difference can always be reasoned through to the satisfaction of all parties.

Nonetheless, the necessary ingredients are present in applied communicative action. Because participants are fully heard as equal and autonomous individuals, the "distortions and coercive elements that characterize so much of our normal day-to-day interaction can be filtered out" (Collins, 1991, p. 12). Consequently communicative action emerges as a useful critical postmodern intervention, whether assisting in fostering discussion or defusing conflict. It leads to a "worthwhile state of affairs that adult educators can seek in a wide variety of contexts. It entails a predisposition towards decision-making processes where all participants are engaged in rational discourse that emerges from a genuinely democratic situation" (p. 12).

Justice

If adult education is instrumental in social and economic advancement, as I have argued throughout this book, we should be able to wager that it places high on society's list of priorities (Husen, 1986; Jarvis, 1987b). Assuming for a moment this is true, it should fare equally well in evoking academic support. Strangely enough, we almost always discover that, regardless of how progressive or provincial, socialistic or laissez-faire, most societies view the formal education of adults well below the attention paid to the maintenance of their health or, for that matter, the resources allocated to schooling for children. In a deplorable irony, though adults comprise our primary source of skilled labor, we invest the least in this group's continued learning and development.

British andragogist Ronald Paterson explores this contradiction in *Values, Education, and the Adult* (1979). Paterson bluntly argues that justice—the binding element in free society—is unattainable when citizens, particularly adults, are refused the opportunity to grow through learning. He convincingly states that democratic cultures have an obligation to provide educational opportunities to adults. Colleges and universities, as both enactors of social policy and cultural guardians, have a clear mandate to help adults become all that their talents might allow.

Educational justice, then, translates into the process by which mature persons have the liberty to pursue educational plans with the consent and blessing of society and its institutions. Further, academic institutions are duty-bound to provide for adults, along with other disadvantaged populations, in meeting a larger mission of eradicating inequality. Their resistance to model justice might well stem from the fact that, internally, many colleges themselves struggle under "authoritarian managements" (Collins, 1991, p. 103). Thus guaranteeing justice for students, particularly those at a class disadvantage, seems even more remote. Adults students must be assured the same opportunity as youth to realize their potential through sponsored learning opportunities, and the university is the logical host.

Finally, educational justice as depicted thus far should not be viewed as a bane to academic institutions or a threat to academic quality (Cross, 1981). Instead, it should be a philosophical "fait accompli" in assemblages dedicated to cultural democracy. In the end, if justice is to flourish, it must be internalized in the people and processes that make up our academic institutions.

IS CAMPUS COMMUNITY REALIZABLE?

In the postmodern age, the concept of community surfaces as an idyll. Since postmodernism is characterized by an "ineradicable plurality" (Baumann, 1991, p. 88) of viewpoints and politics, the constitution of a community with so diverse a set of persons and cultures may be unattainable.

Yet the pursuit of community is one we in academe cannot relinquish. Perhaps because of its ancestry in the sequestered learning enclave of the Middle Ages (Rudolph, 1962), many of today's leaders in higher education still revere this ideal. But today, academic institutions are of a decidedly different nature. They have much more in common with modern cities in their infinite diversity than they do with the walled medieval town or rural colleges of colonial America.

Undoubtedly, there are psychological implications as well. For in a postmodern landscape rife with fragmentation, the vision of community is strangely alluring (Wong, 1991). As is typically human, we long for precisely those things that tend to be the most unreachable. In reading newspapers, watching the evening news, or listening to politicians, we are often blitzed by a fusillade of sound bites warning us of civilization's impending collapse. In so uncertain a world, it is no wonder we look for sanctuary in our personal and social lives.

And the past is difficult to let go. Many prominent educators decry the digression of higher education from its proud heritage. Some are adamant in blaming the demise of that golden era on the influx of adult students whose entry altered the complexion of the campus. Carnegie Commission fellow Ernest Boyer speaks to these issues in *Campus Life: In Search of Community* (1990, pp. 3–4):

Further, lots of older people now populate the campus. . . . Often they enroll part-time, only attend a class or two each week, and because of complicated schedules, they are unable to participate fully in campus life. Given these profound changes in the composition of today's student body, administrators are now asking: Is it even realistic to talk about community in higher education when students have changed so much and their commitments are so divided?

The cynicism of old guard thinking seeps through such rhetoric: the status quo has been compromised by the arrival of adults on campus. To the postmodernist, Boyer's views read like a defense of academe as a cultural museum (Tierney, 1993), a preserve of knowledge and civilization threatened by adult hordes who are massing at the gates. To those sharing his sentiments, academic community is a thing to be remembered and revered as paradise lost, while recreating it with contemporary student enrollments is simply incomprehensible.

Thankfully, there are others, the next generation of academic leaders, who feel differently. They believe that, in spite of dramatic individual and cultural differences, we all share two things that unite us: a reviling of social inequity and our craving for a respectful and safe environment where we can come together and learn without distrust, bigotry, or fear. Livingston and Berger (1994, p. 429) describe such a campus, one thoughtfully crafted and motivated by agape:

We chose to create an organization called the University at Albany Coalition for a Just Community. The Coalition is composed of students, faculty, and staff who care deeply about this kind of university in which they carry out their academic and social lives. The purpose of this coalition was to develop a set of ideas and principles around which all groups . . . could structure their lives, and equally important, feel a strong sense of commitment to their development and preservation.

Though neither author describes himself as a theorist, the vision they inspire is purely critical postmodern. It asks faculty, staff, and students to rally around an idea that benefits the lot of each and improves campus life for all. Not only does it promise participants certain rewards, it also obliges them to help the dream become realized. The essence of the critical postmodern community is responsibility. Nonetheless, in spite of its idealized language and ambition, these authors are not so giddy as to rule out the conflict that arises from heterogeneity. That too, however, they tackle with aplomb: "Instead of ignoring the conflict that comes with diversity or attempting to regulate it through restrictive codes of conduct, we chose to create a set of positive ideals that are now the 'common ground' for all groups, a common ethos for faculty, staff and students—the Principle of a Just Community" (p. 429). The authors explore these principles—equality, liberty, and justice—for their learning applications. While doubters might chide the utopian tone of their article, serious attempts to translate their vision into practice at SUNY-Albany have been made and have met with success.

Mitchel Livingston recently came to the University of Cincinnati as student affairs vice-president. One of his first official actions was establishing a university-wide initiative for building community. The principle he chose to build upon was justice. At the time of this writing, his plan is still in its early stages and is gathering momentum as it reaches different and disparate enclaves. Where heard, it has been warmly greeted and has galvanized support throughout student, faculty, and administrative cadres.

The Eclipsing of Renegade Individualism

For community to grow as a campus ideal with cross-cultural appeal, academic leaders must stave off the contagion of me-ism and the individual rights obsession that ultimately infected modernity's view of social harmony (Falk, 1988). As we have witnessed in late twentieth-century national and partisan politics, a sense of civic pride and duty is impossible to instill when all participants are unyielding in matters of personal interest. Bennis (1989, p. 40) hits the mark: "The conflicts between individual rights and the common good are far older than the nation, but they have never been as sharp or as mean as they are today. In fact, as the upwardly mobile person has replaced the citizen, we have less and less in common and less and less that is good."

Critical postmodernism extends the goals of modernism into a theoretical currency for change (Usher, 1994). One hopes that society learned something from the frenetic ascension of individuality over the collective. The by-product of this frenzy was the loss of social consciousness and responsibility, or the "hollowing of America" (Etzioni, 1983, p. 3) into a land without common purpose. What we propose now is simply to restore the balance. Persons can and must retain their uniqueness in the cultural mosaic that is contemporary America, yet accept the fact that with guaranteed personal freedoms come concurrent obligations. Social duty is the essence of critical postmodern politics.

In these times, the reconciliation of individual rights with accountability must be recovered. As Naisbett and Aburdene (1990, p. 299) observed of the postmodern "new age ":

This is not an every man for himself type of individualism, gratifying one's desires for their own sake and to hell with everyone else. It is an ethical philosophy that elevates the individual to the global level; we all are responsible for preserving the environment, preventing nuclear warfare, eliminating poverty . . . When people satisfy genuine achievement needs, society gains.

Rampant individualism precipitated the decay of communities. Critical postmodernism tells us that the former must decrease so the latter can rebound. What is needed, then, is an ethical stewardship, or moral moderation to check individualism while simultaneously restoring our concern for the community. Gene Outka asserted a similar sentiment in *Agape: An Ethical Analysis* (1972). The idea is incandescent: adopting an overarching, moral concern that animates our thoughts, deeds, and intentions in encountering the community and each other. In sum, we have an obligation to improve rather than manipulate or destroy the personal and social contracts we form with others. Regardless of the site of interaction—classroom, church, voting booth—we must act on a legitimate concern for the greater social good.

Adult Educators as "Communitarians"

The seeds of a grassroots movement recognizing the need to break away from modernism's wanton individualism have been planted. The burgeoning "communitarian" dialogue (Frohnen, 1996; Kahne, 1996) helped fertilize this soil, projecting a future where each member of society develops a personal identity directly linked to and strengthened by his or her contributions to the neighborhood, city, and nation they inhabit. Over time, then, self-interest gives way to involvement in the community.

The core of communitarian philosophy is plain: "The individual and the community make each other and require each other" (Etzioni, 1988, p. 9). They can survive separately, but they will flourish only in close cooperation. Further, "Individuals may pull to diminish the community; the community may pull excessively to incorporate individuals. But if neither element gains ascendancy and if the excesses of one are corrected by shoring up the other, a balanced responsive community may be sustained." Thus, while a "creative tension" (Etzioni, 1983, p. 20) characterizes the relationship, it nonetheless forges ahead in a "continuous search for balance, not the domination of one by the other." Critical postmodern education encapsulates the very same ideal in granting that friction will occur on today's campus but that no one need be forgotten or silenced in the common quest for learning community.

According to its chief architect, Amitai Etzioni, the pendulum swing back toward communitarianism was inescapable. Historically, the phenomenon is simply "the next step in a dialectical progression that started with traditionalism, moved through a retreat from society, and is now ripe for a third stage, that of reconstruction of individuals and community" (1983, p. 27). The historical periods implied here are the premodern, modern, postmodern. Though linked to contemporary times, communitarianism defies physical boundaries and may be seen in institutional as well as public spaces.

Because they are often fragmented politically and prone to subcultural grouping, with many of them clamoring for entitlements due them as distinct and deserving factions of individuals, colleges and universities are natural sites for experimenting with communitarian principles. After all, the postmodern academy changed to comply with the rising student demand for a voice in governance. As Holland (1988, p. 59) noted, "participation is becoming more direct, more organic, less hierarchical, less bureaucratic." As long as the increased participation brings with it a concomitant expectation of responsible action on everyone's part, the interests of democracy and community will still be served.

Instead of squabbling internally for prestige and resources by asserting their automatic "right" to both, academic leaders should demonstrate their programs' value to the larger community (Kerr, 1994) by remembering the pledge made to those most in need of access to learning. Where adults are concerned, the need for institutional responsibility is especially intense. Leaders in community and adult education services, then, should spearhead these efforts.

SUMMARY

A mystique continues to envelop leadership. The stuff of which it is made is simultaneously magical, yearned for, and yet esoteric. We know the qualities "good" leaders possess (Fisher and Tack, 1988), but the equation for producing them remains a mystery.

If the ingredients for transformative leadership are unknown, perhaps we can at least speculate our way to a recipe. Perhaps some provocative ideas for discovering such a path have been set forth in this discussion. If not, let me briefly restate my position. Leadership, above all else, focuses on drawing people into decision making and treating them as equals. From this rather mundane prescription, new worlds have been built. Tierney (1993, p. 23) expresses the same sentiment more eloquently:

To be clear: dialogues of hope enable people to come together to define common and conflicting purposes, desires, and wants. . . . In a postmodern democratic community, conflict is inevitable and utopias will never be reached. And yet, having said that, I also am suggesting that some form of meaning must exist, otherwise we live a passionless world at the least, and at worst, we inhabit a nihilistic one where oppression goes unchecked and untrammeled.

Adult educators properly prepared to lead programs and services effectively for older students comprise another rare breed. As I have argued in this book, for adult education to fulfill its democratic mission and obligation to justice, it cannot ignore the political, social, and cultural factors shaping its existence in the university.

Educators of both an administrative and andragogical bent must cultivate a leadership style recognizing the salience of these factors in the work they undertake. Adult students are different from traditional-age learners in several significant ways, the least of which is their desire for an active voice in the process and content of learning. As a result, standard techniques for instruction and administration have become ineffectual. Instead, what is needed is a fundamental paradigm shift, or "metanoia," one encouraging the formation of a completely new perspective in those who guide adult learning services.

Theory, once again, emerges as an epistemology (way of knowing) for transformation. As it has in many other places within this book, theory ruminates on what could be in a systematic and plausible manner, allowing for multiple futures while shunning simple fancy. Because it is the purest and best-informed of mental exercises, theory contains limitless possibilities. As teachers, deans, or simply lifelong learners in adult education, theory of the critical postmodern variety appears especially suited to grooming new leadership.

Postscript

> It is not so long ago that it was felt that the adult's ability to learn declined with age and that learning was something that mainly happened in childhood. Our education system, together with those of most developed nations, is founded on the premise that childhood is the best time to learn. . . . The assumption is that an initial burst of education can equip a person for life.
> —D. Jones, *Adult Education and Cultural Development* (1988, p. 151)

The persistence of memories like the one above should not be minimized. They are too strongly etched in our educational consciousness to wave off with a sigh and smile of disbelief. In the preceding chapters I have stressed the primacy of tradition in molding ideas about what adult education has been and what it should be.

I conclude this study with some reflections on its social significance. The legacy it hopes to bequeath is one of transformation through enlightenment. Informing educators of the barriers adults face on interpersonal, perceptual, and organizational levels is a key step toward raising awareness. In time, this heightened consciousness of the cultural biases present in academic institutions will prompt a response. If I have been successful in identifying areas where the need for change is most urgent, it is probable that future actions will be appropriately directed and strong enough to eradicate the problems.

Too often in our culture of consumption, we permit the skills and intellectual energies of mature individuals to be squandered as another disposable resource. Society has somehow become bound to the misconception that learning ends with youth—with a little mileage comes rust and decay. British scholar Peter Jarvis laments this mentality that consigns adults to the scrapheap, their accumulated learning and biographies "treated as obsolete—like some many things in this throwaway world" (1992, p. 203). I hope this book has shown that it is time to free ourselves from the fetters of such tragically wasteful thinking.

Dispelling myths that persist about adults' limitations as learners is what this book aspired to do. If, in the process, it makes adult students aware that they merit a place in the university community and can still contribute a verse to the poetry of life, then all the better. Finally, should this research take academic leaders and those who guard the culture of the academy to new educational frontiers, then it will have attained the author's greatest expectation for it.

The dawn of empowerment for any ascendant group is recognition of worth. However, this knowledge must first be internalized in the person. It is up to educators to nurture this sense of legitimacy, place, and power. This very need continues to make critical scholarship and transformative educators relevant (Mooney, 1992). Once accomplished, adult education programs can begin moving from the periphery to the center of campus life. Ultimately, the rise of any disadvantaged population in an institution purported to be as subservient to democracy as the university has larger social implications. With this in mind, I have attempted to construct a narrative to serve as a staging ground for the movement to commence.

To return to the research question that guided these analyses: based on available information, academic and anecdotal, are colleges and universities meeting the cultural needs of the adult students they claim to serve? Sufficient data has been amassed in the preceding chapters to lend credibility to the thesis that adults are, albeit to alternating degrees, "at-risk" in traditional higher education. While I might be hesitant to state that my arguments have been supported to the point of generalizability, this was never my intention. This work aspired to point out the philosophical contradictions and programmatic half-truths currently hindering adult education. Further, it employed critical and postmodern theory to explore these aspects of adult education philosophy and practice in a way that standard methodologies simply could not. To that end, this researcher is satisfied.

When all is said and done, however, we need to recall that all rhetoric, polemics, and theorizing aside, what is at stake are the lives of mature human beings and their inherent potential. If we agree on this premise, it is imperative for us to introduce a "language of possibility" (Aronowitz and Giroux, 1985) when speculating about the future of adult education and the array of students whom it serves. Concomitantly, we must transcend the inclination of critical theory to rest at simply uncovering inequality. As Apple implores: "We need to recognize the positive, not just the negative, relationship between power and knowledge" (1989, p. 177). Only at this stage can we contemplate an educational program of grander dimensions.

It is also necessary that we finally bury, no matter how wistfully, antiquated methods of analysis for apprehending the complex layers of human experience around us—physical, social, and cultural. Procedures for investigation developed centuries ago cannot explain the multicultural, technologically imprinted world in which we now live. Their interment is overdue. If mainstream scholarship had become less preoccupied with its own calculus earlier, we might not feel so powerless to do anything with the reams of data gathered and then mothballed over the years. Where such knowledge—had it been tempered with qualitative insight—might have been used to improve our social surroundings and relationships is a particularly bittersweet musing.

Distancing themselves from tradition, critical theories denounce venerated research models for their proclivity to dehumanize, sterilize, and objectify different groups and the cultures they create. In the final translation, these propensities keep disadvantaged peoples in the margins and muffle their discourses in the name of preserving academic integrity.

At the same time, however, I did not want to risk losing my reader by waxing too abstract. Theory may be incredibly instructive, but predisposed toward unbearable tedium if not grounded in the familiar. Greenleaf (1991, p. 5) says it better:

Criticism has its place; but as a total preoccupation it is sterile. In a time of crisis, like the leadership crisis we are now in, if too many potential builders are taken in by a complete absorption with dissecting the wrong and by a zeal for instant perfection, then the movement so many of us want to see will be set back. The danger perhaps, is to *hear the analysts too much and the artists too little*. [italics added]

Throughout this book, I have tried to balance theoretical insight with concrete examples so the reader might understand how theory becomes actual. Illustrations taken from the literature, from the stories of older students, and from my own professional experiences were provided to support the practical goals of this project. Connected to my desire for pragmatism was a coincidental concern for humanity. The issues treated and the problems identified became a little more painful, a bit more urgent when I invested more of myself into the discussion of educational questions than might otherwise seem routine. Perhaps as a counterweight to the theorizing, this device made for a more appealing discussion but perhaps also showed something else in blazing an alternative trail for qualitative research.

The detached indifference demanded by traditional empiricism has led to the abysmal state in which we find ourselves. As researchers and clinicians we are trained to set aside subjective reaction. No matter how grave the problem or troubling the phenomenon, we are asked not to feel. Scholarship strictly forbids the expression of personality in our writings. Page Smith, offered a lighthearted anecdote in *Killing the Spirit* (1990, pp. 110–111):

It was as a candidate for the Ph.D. at Harvard that I first encountered the Cult of Dullness. Since boyhood I had aspired to be a writer. I was not sure what kind of writer, but some kind. So with my first graduate research paper I tried to write as well as I could. My professor, the urbane Crane Brinton, warned me gently that although he did not object to a well-written paper. . . his colleagues might be put off. They might suspect that I was not really committed to dull writing (he didn't put it exactly that way) and thus not a suitable candidate for the Ph.D.

His levity is appreciated, but not more than the message he conveys: humanness should have a place in academic writing. Something of the author should shine through the charts, data, and synopses, otherwise even the most brilliant work falls victim to the Cult of Dullness and loses readers who might be moved as well as enlightened by the material presented.

Consider how easily we regard welfare recipients as a vast cohort of faceless numbers on government lists rather than human beings living a life of despair in poverty. A more poignant example is the gang violence among African-American youth in inner cities, analyzed with exactness by the social scientist crunching teen mortality rates on supercomputers at the university with little thought to the staggering loss of whose sons and daughters it is that have perished.

True to form, I hope, this book remained eminently readable. As stated at the outset, if this narrative is indecipherable to all but a handful of critical and postmodern theorists, or the language conceptually obscure enough to discourage a broader audience, I will consider it a

Bibliography

ACSCU-WASC. (1994). *Dialogues for Diversity: Community and Ethnicity on Campus*. Accrediting Commission for Senior Colleges and Universities of the Western Association of Schools and Colleges. Phoenix: Oryx Press.

Adams, R. M. (1993). "Religious Ethics in a Pluralistic Society." In G. Outka and J. Reeder, eds., *Prospects for a Common Morality*, 93–113. Princeton, N.J.: Princeton University Press.

Adorno, T. (1967). "The Culture Industry Reconsidered." *Ohne Leitbild*. Frankfurt: Suhrkamp.

_____. (1977). "The Actuality of Philosophy." *Telos* 31 (Spring): 120–133.

Agger, B. (1989). *Fast Capitalism: A Critical Theory of Significance*. Urbana: University of Illinois Press.

_____. (1991). *A Critical Theory of Public Life: Knowledge, Discourse, and Politics in an Age of Decline*. New York: The Falmer Press.

Ahmed, A. S. (1992). *Postmodernism and Islam: Predicament and Promise*. London: Routledge.

Allaire, Y. and M. E. Firsirotu. (1984). "Theories of Organizational Culture." *Organization Studies*. 5: 193–226.

Altbach, P., and R. Berdahl, eds. (1981). *Higher Education in American Society*. Buffalo: Prometheus.

Althusser, L. (1972). "Ideology and the Ideological State Apparatus." In B. R. Cosin, ed., *Education, Structure and Society*. Harmondsworth: Penguin Books.

Anzuldua, G. (1987). *Borderlands: La Frontera*. San Francisco: Spinsters/Aunt Lute.

Apple, M. W. (1989). *Teachers and Texts: A Political Economy of Class and Gender Relations in Education*. New York: Routledge.

Apps, J. (1981). *The Adult Learner on Campus*. Chicago: Follett.

Aronowitz, S. (1981). *The Crisis in Historical Materialism: Class, Politics, and Culture in Marxist Theory.* New York: Praeger.

———. (1988). *Science as Power: Discourse and Ideology in Modern Society.* Minneapolis: University of Minnesota Press.

Aronowitz, S., and H. Giroux. (1991). *Postmodern Education: Politics, Culture, and Social Criticism.* Minneapolis: University of Minnesota Press.

———. (1993). *Education Still under Siege.* Westport, Conn. Bergin and Garvey.

Awkward, M. (1995). *Negotiating Difference: Race, Gender and the Politics of Positionality.* Chicago: University of Chicago Press.

Bagnall. R. (1995). "Discriminative Justice and Responsibility in Postmodernist Adult Education." *Adult Education Quarterly* 45 (2): 79–94.

Bandyopadhyay, P. (1986). "Theoretical Approaches to the State and Social Reproduction." In J. Dickinson and R. Russell, eds., *Family, Economy and State,* 192–222. New York: St. Martin's Press.

Bannet, E. T. (1993). *Postcultural Theory: Critical Theory after the Marxist Paradigm.* New York: Paragon.

Baudrillard, J. (1988). *Selected Writings.* Stanford: Stanford University Press.

———. (1994). *Simulacra and Simulations.* Ann Arbor: University of Michigan Press.

Bauman, Z. (1991). *Modernity and Ambivalence.* Cambridge: Polity Press.

Becker, G. (1975). *Human Capital: A Theoretical and Empirical Analysis with Special Reference to Education.* New York: Columbia University Press.

Bennis, W. (1969). *Organizational Development: Its Nature, Origins and Prospects.* Reading, Mass.: Addison-Wesley.

———. (1976). *The Unconscious Conspiracy: Why Leaders Can't Lead.* New York: AMACOM.

———. (1984). "Transformative Power and Leadership." In T. Sergiovanni and J. Corbally, eds., *Leadership and Organizational Culture: New Perspectives on Administrative Theory and Practice,* 64–71. Urbana: University of Illinois Press.

———. (1985). *The Planning of Change.* New York: Holt, Rinehart, and Winston.

———. (1989). *Why Leaders Can't Lead: The Unconscious Conspiracy Continues.* San Francisco: Jossey-Bass.

———. (1993). *An Invented Life: Reflections on Leadership and Change.* Reading, Mass.: Addison-Wesley.

———. (1994). *Beyond Leadership: Balancing Economics, Ethics, and Ecology.* Cambridge, Mass.: Blackwell.

Bensimon, B., A. Newmann, and F. Birnbaum. (1989). *Making Sense of Administrative Leadership: The "L" Word in Higher Education.* ASHE-ERIC Higher Education Reports. Washington, D.C.: Association for the Study of Higher Education.

Berle, A. and G. Means. (1932). *The Modern Corporation and Private Property.* New York: Commerce Clearing House.

Berube, M. (1994). *Public Access: Literary Theory and American Cultural Politics.* New York: Verso.

Bledstein, B. (1976). *The Culture of Professionalism.* New York: Norton.

Bloom, A. (1987). *The Closing of the American Mind.* New York: Simon and Schuster.

Bok, D. (1982). *Beyond the Ivory Tower: Social Responsibilities of the Modern University.* Cambridge, Mass.: Harvard University Press.

Bowen, H. (1980). *The Costs of Higher Education.* San Francisco: Jossey-Bass.

Bowles, S., and H. Gintis. (1976). *Schooling in Capitalist America.* New York: Basic Books.

Boyer, E. (1990). *Campus Life: In Search of Community.* The Carnegie Foundation for the Advancement of Teaching with a foreword by Ernest Boyer. Princeton: The Foundation.

Branstadter, J. (1984). "Personal and Social Control over Development: Some Implications of an Action Perspective in Life-Span Development." In P. Baltes and O. Grim, eds., *Life Span Development and Behavior,* vol. 6. San Diego: Academic Press.

Bronner, S., and D. Kellner, eds. (1989). *Critical Theory and Society: A Reader.* London: Routledge, Chapman and Hall.

Brookfield. S. (1983). *Adult Learners, Adult Education, and the Community.* New York: Teachers College.

———. (1985). *Self-Directed Learning: From Theory to Practice.* San Francisco: Jossey-Bass.

———. (1986). *Understanding and Facilitating Adult Learning.* San Francisco: Jossey-Bass.

Carnegie Commission. (1973). *Toward a Learning Society: Alternative Channels to Life, Work, and Service.* New York: McGraw-Hill.

Carnevale, A. (1983). "Higher Education's Role in the American Economy." *Educational Record* 64 (Fall): 6–16.

———. (1991). *America and the New Economy.* Alexandria, Va.: American Society for Training and Development; U.S. Department of Labor.

Cervero, R. (1988). *Effective Continuing Education for Professionals.* San Francisco: Jossey-Bass.

Chickering, A. (1981). *The Modern American College.* San Francisco: Jossey-Bass.

Chickering, A., and R. Havighurst. (1981). "The Life Cycle." in A. Chickering, ed., *The Modern American College,* 16–50. San Francisco: Jossey-Bass.

Chin, R., and K. Benne. (1985). "General Strategies for Effecting Change in Human Systems." In W. Bennis, *The Planning of Change,* 22–45. New York: Holt.

Chism, N., J. Cano, and A. Pruitt. (1989). "Teaching in a Diverse Environment: Knowledge and Skills Needed by TAs." In J. Nyquist and R. Abbott, eds., *Teaching Assistant Training in the 1990's*, 23–36. New Directions for Teaching and Learning 39. San Francisco: Jossey-Bass.

Chronicle of Higher Education. (1996). *Almanac Issue* 43 (1) (September 2).

Cianciolo, M. (1995). "Guinier: Majority Rule Not True Democracy." *University Currents* (University of Cincinnati) 4 (16; February 3): 3.

Clark, M. C. (1993). "Transformational Learning." In S. Merriam, *An Update on Adult Learning Theory*, 47–56. New Directions for Adult and Continuing Education 57 (Spring). San Francisco: Jossey-Bass.

Cohen, S. (1993). *Academia and the Lustre of Capital*. Minneapolis: University of Minnesota Press.

Collins, M. (1991). *Adult Education as Vocation: A Critical Role for the Adult Educator*. London: Routledge.

Crane, J. M. (1987). "Moses Coady and Antigonish." In P. Jarvis, ed. *Twentieth Century Thinkers in Adult Education*, 217–242. London: Croom Helm.

Crook, S. (1992). *Postmodernization: Change in Advanced Society*. London: Sage.

Cross, K. P. (1971). *Beyond the Open Door*. San Francisco: Jossey-Bass.

——— . (1981). *Adults as Learners*. San Francisco: Jossey-Bass.

Delahaye, B., D. Limerick, and G. Hearn. (1994). "The Relationship between Andragogical and Pedagogical Orientations and the Implications for Adult Learning." *Adult Education Quarterly* 44 (4): 187–198.

Delworth, U., and G. Hanson. (1989). *Student Services: A Handbook for the Profession*, 2nd ed. San Francisco: Jossey-Bass.

Dewey, J. (1916). *Democracy and Education: An Introduction to the Philosophy of Education*. New York: The Free Press.

Dews, P. (1987). *Logics of Disintegration: Post-Structuralist Thought and the Claims of Critical Theory*. London: Verso.

Dickens, D., ed. (1994). *Postmodernism and Social Inquiry*. New York: Guilford Press.

Dickinson, J., and R. Russell, eds. (1986). *Family, Economy and State: The Social Reproduction Process under Capitalism*. New York: St. Martins Press.

Dillman, D., J. Christenson, P. Salant, and P. Warner. (1995). *What the Public Wants from Higher Education: Workforce Implications from a 1995 National Survey*. Social and Economic Sciences Research Center. Washington State University. Pullman: SESR.

Donagan, A. (1993). "Common Morality and Kant's Enlightenment Project." In G. Outka and J. Reeder, eds., *Prospects for a Common Morality*, 53–72. Princeton: Princeton University Press.

D'Souza, D. (1991). *Illiberal Education: The Politics of Race and Sex on Campus*. New York: The Free Press.

Edelson, P., ed. (1992). *Rethinking Leadership in Adult and Continuing Education.* New Directions for Adult and Continuing Education 56. San Francisco: Jossey-Bass.

Elliott, P. G. (1994). *The Urban Campus: Educating the New Majority for the New Century.* American Council on Education. Phoenix: Oryx Press.

Ellsworth, E. (1989). "Why Doesn't This Feel Empowering? Working through the Repressive Myth of Critical Pedagagogy." *Harvard Educational Review* 59 (3): 297–324.

Etzioni, A. (1983). *An Immodest Agenda: Rebuilding America before the Twenty-First Century.* New York: McGraw Hill.

———. (1988). *The Moral Dimension: Toward a New Economics.* New York: The Free Press.

Fairweather, J. (1988). *Entrepreneurship and Higher Education:* Lessons for Colleges, Universities, and Industry. ASHE-ERIC Higher Education Report 6. Washington: ASHE.

———. (1991). "Managing Industry-University Research Relationships." *Journal for Higher Education Management* 6 (2): 7–14.

Falk, R. A. (1990). "In Pursuit of the Postmodern." In D. Griffin, ed., *Spirituality and Society: Postmodern Visions,* 81–98. Albany: State University of New York Press.

Fay, B. (1987). *Critical Social Science: Liberation and Its Limits.* Ithaca. N.Y.: Cornell University Press.

Fisher, J., and M. Tack, eds. (1988). *Leaders on Leadership: The College Presidency.* New Directions for Higher Education 61 (Spring). San Francisco: Jossey-Bass.

Foucault, M. (1973). "The Intellectuals and Power." *Telos* 16: 103–109.

———. (1980). *Power/Knowledge: Selected Interviews and Other Writings.* New York: Pantheon.

Fox, C. (1995). *Postmodern Public Administration.* Thousand Oaks, Calif.: Sage Publications.

Freiberg, J. W., ed. (1979). *Critical Sociology: European Perspectives.* New York: Irvington.

Freire, P. (1972a). *The Pedagogy of the Oppressed.* London: Penguin.

———. (1972b). *Cultural Action for Freedom.* London: Penguin.

———. (1973). "Before They Can Teach." *Convergence* 6 (1).

Frohnen, B. (1996). *The New Communitarians and the Crisis of Modern Liberalism.* Lawrence: University of Kansas Press.

Galbraith, J. K. (1992). *The Culture of Contentment.* Boston: Houghton Miflin.

Gelpi, E. (1985). *Lifelong Education and International Relations.* London: Croom Helm.

Gergen, K. J. (1991). *The Saturated Self: Dilemmas of Identity in Contemporary Life.* New York: Basic Books.

Giddens, A. (1979). "Habermas on Hermeneutics." in J. W. Freiberg, ed., *Critical Sociology*, 39–71. New York: Irvington.

Giroux, H. (1982). *Theory and Resistance in Education*. Boston: Bergin and Garvey.

———. (1988a). *Schooling and the Struggle for Public Life: Critical Pedagogy in the Modern Age*. Minneapolis: University of Minnesota Press.

———. (1988b). "Border Pedagogy in the Age of Postmodernism." *Journal of Education* 170 (3): 162–181.

———. (1990). "The Politics of Postmodernism." *Journal of Urban and Cultural Studies* 1 (1): 5–38.

———. (1992). *Border Crossings: Cultural Workers and the Politics of Education*. New York: Routledge.

Gold, L. N. (1992). "Improving College Access for Needy Adults Under Existing Federal Programs." *Financing Nontraditional Students: A Seminar Report*, 33–46. Washington: ACE.

Gramsci, A. (1971). *Selections from a Prison Notebook*. New York: International Publishers.

Grattan, C. Hartley. (1959). *American Ideas about Adult Education: 1710–1951*. New York: Teacher's College Press.

Greenleaf, R. (1972). *The Institution as Servant*. Indianapolis: Robert K. Greenleaf Center.

———. (1979). *Teacher as Servant: A Parable*. Indianapolis: Robert K. Greenleaf Center.

———. (1991). *The Servant as Leader*, expanded from 1970 ed. Indianapolis: Robert K. Greenleaf Center.

Griffin, D., ed. (1988). *Spirituality and Society: Postmodern Visions*. Albany: State University of New York Press.

Gumport, P. (1991). "The Research Imperative." In W. Tierney, ed., *Culture and Ideology in Higher Education*, 87–106. New York: Praeger.

Habermas, J. (1987). *The Philosophical Discourse of Modernity*. Cambridge, Mass.: Massachusetts Institute of Technology Press.

———. (1992). *Autonomy and Solidarity*. London: Verso.

Hart, M. (1990). "Critical Theory and Beyond: Further Perspectives on Emancipatory Education." *Adult Education Quarterly* 40 (3): 125–138.

Heaney, T. (1989). *Struggling to Be Free*. Dekalb: Lindeman Center, Northern Illinois University.

———. (1992). "When Adult Education Stood for Democracy." *Adult Education Quarterly* 43 (1): 51–59.

———. (1993). "Identifying and Dealing with Educational, Social, and Political Issues." In *Administration of Adult Education Programs*, 13–20. New Directions for Adult and Continuing Education 60 (Winter). San Francisco: Jossey Bass.

Hearn, F. (1973). "The Implications of Critical Theory for Critical Sociology." *Berkeley Journal of Sociology* 18: 127–58.

Heerman, B. (1976). *Changing Managerial Perspectives.* San Francisco: Jossey-Bass.

Heerman, B., C. Enders, and E. Wine, eds. (1980). *Serving Lifelong Learners.* San Francisco: Jossey-Bass.

Hegel, G. W. (1912). *Doctrine of Formal Logic.* Oxford: Clarendon Press.

Held, D. (1980). *Introduction to Critical Theory: Horkheimer to Habermas.* Berkeley: University of California Press.

Heller, S. (1995). "A Nimble Advocate for the Left in the Culture Wars." *Chronicle of Higher Education* 41 (22): 6–12.

Hesburgh, T. (1988). "Academic Leadership." In J. Fisher and M. Tack, eds., *Leaders on Leadership: The College Presidency,* 6–8. New Directions for Higher Education 61 (Spring). San Francisco: Jossey-Bass.

Hicks, E. (1988). "Deterritorialization and Border Writing." In R. Merill, ed., *Ethics/Aesthetics: Post-modern Positions,* 47–58. Washington D.C.: Maisonneuve.

Hill, P. J. (1991). "Multiculturalism: The Crucial Philosophical and Organizational Issues." *Change* 23 (4): 38–47.

Hill, S. (1991). "Ethnicity: Identity and Difference." *Radical America* 13 (4): 9–20.

Hirsch, E. D. (1987). *Cultural Literacy: What Every American Needs to Know.* Boston: Houghton Miflin.

Holford, J. (1995). "Why Social Movements Matter: Adult Education Theory, Cognitive Praxis, and the Creation of Knowledge." *Adult Education Quarterly* 45 (2): 95–111.

Holland, J. (1990). "A Postmodern Vision of Spirituality and and Society." In D. Griffin, ed. *Spirituality and Society: Postmodern Visions,* 41–62. Albany: State University of New York Press.

Holmes, G. (1995). Adult Education Needs a Louder Voice. *Adult Learning* 6 (6): 14–19.

hooks, b. (1984). *Feminist Theory from Margin to Center.* Boston: South End Press.

Horkheimer, M. (1972). "Authority and the Family." In M. J. O'Connell, *Critical Theory,* New York: Herder.

———. (1974). *Eclipse of Reason.* New York: Seabury Press.

Hu-Dehart, E. (1995). "Reconceptualizing Liberal Education: The Importance of Ethnic Studies." *Educational Record* 76 (2/3): 22–33.

Hull, M. (1992). "University Planning and Budget Reductions." *Journal of Higher Education Management* 8 (1): 13–18.

Husen, T. (1986). *The Learning Society Revisited.* New York: Pergamon Press.

Ilsey, P. (1992). "The Undeniable Link: Adult and Continuing Education and Social Change." *New Directions in Adult and Continuing Education* 53 (Spring): 25–37.

Jacobs, N. (1989). "Nontraditional Students: The New Ecology of the Classroom." *Educational Forum* 53: 330–336.

Jameson, F. (1991). *Postmodernism: The Cultural Logic of Late Capitalism.* Durham: Duke University Press.

Jarvis, P. (1987a). *Adult Learning in the Social Context.* New York: Croom Helm.

———. (1987b). *Twentieth Century Thinkers in Adult Education.* Beckenham, UK: Croom Helm.

———. (1992). *Paradoxes of Learning: On Becoming an Individual Society.* San Francisco: Jossey-Bass.

Jeria, J. (1990). "Popular Education: Models That Contribute to the Empowerment of Learners in Minority Communities." In *Serving Culturally Diverse Populations. New Directions in Adult and Continuing Education* 48: 93–100.

Jones, D. (1988). *Adult Education and Cultural Development.* New York: Routledge.

Jonsen, A. R. (1991). "Of Balloons and Bicycles." *Hastings Center Report* (September/October): 14–17.

Kahne, J. (1996). *Reframing Educational Policy: Democracy, Community, and the Individual.* New York: Teacher's College Press.

Kanpol, B. (1992). *Towards a Theory and Practice of Teacher Cultural Politics: Continuing the Postmodern Debate.* Norwood, N.J.: Ablex.

Kaplan, C. (1987). *Scattered Hegemonies: Postmodernity and Transnational Feminist Practices.* Minneapolis: University of Minnesota Press.

Karol, N. and S. Ginsburg. (1980). *Managing the Higher Education Enterprise.* New York: Wiley and Sons.

Kellner, D. (1989). *Jean Baudrillard: From Marxism to PostModernism and Beyond.* Stanford: Stanford University Press.

Kellner, D., and R. Roderick. (1981). "Recent Literature on Critical Theory." *New German Critique* 23 (Spring/Summer): 141–70.

Kempner, K. (1991). "Understanding Cultural Conflict." In W. Tierney, ed., *Culture and Ideology in Higher Education*, 129–150. New York: Praeger.

Kerr, C. (1963). *The Uses of the University.* Cambridge, Mass.: Harvard University Press.

———. (1994). *Troubled Times for American Higher Education.* Albany: State University of New York Press.

King, M. L. (1958). *Stride toward Freedom.* New York: Harper & Row.

Knowles, M. (1984). *Andragogy in Action.* San Francisco: Jossey-Bass.

———. (1990). *The Adult Learner: A Neglected Species.* Houston: Gulf Publishing Company.

———. (1995). "Predicting the Future of Higher Education." *Network* (Cincinnati: The Union Institute) 12 (2): 23–25.

Knox, A. (1986). *Helping Adults Learn.* San Francisco: Jossey-Bass.

Kothari, R. (1983). "Survival in an Age of Transformation." *Praxis International* 2 (4): 371–388.

Kouzes, J., and B. Posner. (1987). *The Leadership Challenge: How to Get Extraordinary Things Done in Organizations.* San Francisco: Jossey-Bass.

Kuh, G. (1990). "Organizational Concepts and Influences." In U. Delworth and G. Hanson, eds., *Student Services: A Handbook for the Profession.* 209–242. San Francisco: Jossey-Bass.

Laclau, E. (1988). "Politics and the Limits of Modernity." In A. Ross, ed., *Universal Abandon? The Politics of Postmodernism,* Minneapolis: University of Minnesota Press.

Laclau, E., and C. Mouffe. (1985). *Hegemony and Socialist Strategy.* London: Verso.

Laidlaw, A. (1961). *The Campus and the Community: The Global Impact of the Antigonish Movement.* Montreal: Harvest House Limited.

Leiss, W. (1972). "The Critical Theory of Society: Present Situation and Future Tasks." In P. Breines, *Critical Interruptions: New Left Perspectives on Herbert Marcuse.* New York: Continuum Books.

Lincoln, Y. (1991). "Advancing a Critical Agenda." In W. Tierney, ed. *Culture and Ideology in Higher Education,* 17–34. New York: Praeger.

Lindeman, E. (1926). *The Meaning of Adult Education.* New York: New Republic.

Livingston, M., and M. Berger. (1994). "Developing a Coalition and Principles for a Just Community." *The Review of Education/Pedagogy/Cultural Studies* 16 (3/4): 427–433.

Lorde, A. (1984). *Sister Outsider: Essays and Speeches.* Trumansburg, N.Y.: Crossing Press.

Lynch, J., and C. Bishop-Clark. (1994). "The Influence of Age in College Classrooms: Some New Evidence." *Community College Review* 22 (3): 3–12.

Lyotard, J. (1984). *The Postmodern Condition: A Report on Knowledge.* Minneapolis: University of Minnesota Press.

Machlup, F. (1976). *Selected Economic Writings of Fritz Machlup.* New York: New York University Press.

_____. (1984). *Knowledge: Its Creation, Distribution and Economic Significance.* Princeton, N.J.: Princeton University Press.

Marcus, J., and Z. Tar. (1984). *Foundations of the Frankfurt School of Social Research.* New Brunswick, N.J.: Transaction Books.

Marcuse, H. (1963). *Revolution and Reason.* New York: Humanities Press.

_____. (1989a). "Liberation from an Affluent Society." In S. Bronner and D. Kellner, eds., *Critical Theory and Society,* 276–287. London: Routledge.

———. (1989b). "Philosophy and Critical Theory." In S. Bronner and D. Kellner, eds., *Critical Theory and Society*, 58–76. London: Routledge.

———. (1989c). "The Obsolescence of the Freudian Concept of Man." In S. Bronner and D. Kellner, eds., *Critical Theory and Society*, 233–246. London: Routledge.

Matthews, J., and R. Noorgard. (1984). *Managing the Partnership between Higher Education and Industry*. Boulder, Colo.: NCHEMS.

McGaughey, J. (1992). "Symbolic Leadership: Redefining Relationships within the Host Organization." In P. Edelson, ed., *Rethinking Leadership in Adult and Continuing Education*, 39–50. New Directions for Adult and Continuing Education 56. San Francisco: Jossey Bass.

McLaren, P. (1993). *Schooling as a Ritual Performance*, 2nd ed. New York: Routledge.

Metzger, W. (1981). "Acdemic Freedom in Delocalized Academic Institutions." In P. Altbach and R. Berdahl, ed., *Higher Education in American Society*, 55–72. Buffalo: Prometheus.

Miller, D. (1991). *Handbook of Research Design and Social Measurement*, 5th ed. Newbury Park: Sage.

Milner, M. (1972). *The Illusion of Equality*. San Francisco: Jossey-Bass.

Montero, J. (1995). "Safe Space or Separation?: Mediating the Tension." *Educational Record* 76 (2/3): 37–40.

Mooney, C. (1992). "Leftist Scholars in a Post Soviet World." *The Chronicle of Higher Education* 38 (5): 19–21.

Morgan, G. (1986). *Images of Organizations*. Newbury Park, Calif.: Sage Publications.

Mouffe, C. (1988). "Hegemony and New Political Subjects: Toward a New Concept of Democracy." In C. Nelson and L. Grossberg, eds., *Marxism and the Interpretation of Culture*, 89–101. Urbana (IL): University of Illinois Press.

Mounty, L. (1991). "Involving Nontraditional Commuting Students in the Career Planning Process at an Urban Institution." *Journal for Higher Education Management* 6 (2): 43–48.

Naisbett, J., and P. Aburdene. (1990). *Megatrends 2000: Ten New Directions for the 1990s*. New York: Morrow.

Navarro, V. (1979). "Social Class, Political Power, and the State: Their Implications in Medicine." In J. Freiberg, ed., *Critical Sociology*, 297–344. New York: Irvington.

Niblett, W. Roy. (1994). "After the Movement." *Change* 26 (3): 20–21.

Nieto, S. (1992). *Affirming Diversity: The Sociopolitical Context of Multicultural Education*. White Plains, N.Y.: Longman.

NUCEA (1995). "New and Older College Student Profile." National University Continuing Education Association. *NUCEA News* 11 (6): 3.

O'Connor, P. J. (1994). "The Needs of Adult University Students." *College and University* 49 (2): 84–87.

O'Toole, J. (1995). *Leading Change: Overcoming the Ideology of Comfort and the Tyranny of Custom.* San Francisco: Jossey-Bass.

Outka, G. (1972). *Agape: An Ethical Analysis.* New Haven: Yale University Press.

Outka, G., and J. Reeder. (1993). *Prospects for a Common Morality.* Princeton, N.J.: Princeton University Press.

Outlaw, L. (1983). "Critical Theory in a Period of Radical Transformation." *Praxis International* 13 (2): 138–146.

Parnell, D. (1990). *Dateline 2000: The New Higher Education Agenda.* American Association of Community and Junior Colleges. Washington, D.C.: Community College Press.

Paterson, R. (1979). *Values, Education, and the Adult.* Boston: Routledge, Kegan, Paul.

Patton, M. Q. (1990). *Qualitative Evaluations and Research Methods,* 2nd ed. Newbury Park, Calif.: Sage Publications.

Payne, C. (1984). *Getting What We Asked For: The Ambiguity of Success and Failure in Urban Education.* Westport, Conn.: Greenwood Press.

Peters, J. M. (1980). *Building an Effective Adult Education Enterprise.* San Francisco: Jossey-Bass.

Pittman, E. (1994). "Cultural Centers on Predominantly White Campuses." *Black Issues in Higher Education* (October 6): 104.

Poster, M. (1989). *Critical Theory and Poststructuralism.* Ithaca, N.Y.: Cornell University Press.

Pruitt, G. (1988). "Some Good Advice." In J. Fisher and M. Tack, eds., *Leaders on Leadership: The College Presidency.* New Directions for Higher Education. 61 (Spring): 31–35. San Francisco: Jossey-Bass.

Quinnan, T. (1995a). "Mass Opportunity and the GI Bill." In *The End of the Second World War and Its Aftermath: Proceedings.* Los Alamos: Los Alamos Historical Society.

———. (1995b). "Culture, Theory and Leadership." *Black Issues in Higher Education* (March 23): 108.

Ray, L., ed. (1990). *Critical Sociology.* London: Elgar.

Reid, G. (1995). "Mapping the Route to the New Millennium." *Community College Journal* 65 (5): 18–24.

Richardson, R. (1991). *Achieving Quality and Diversity.* New York: American Council on Education.

Riessman, D. (1980). *On Higher Education.* San Francisco: Jossey-Bass.

Rogers, D., and R. Ruchlin. (1971). *Education and Economy:* New York: The Free Press.

Rorty, R. (1989.) *Contingency, Irony, Solidarity.* Cambridge: Cambridge University Press.

Rosaldo, R. (1989). *Culture and Truth: The Remaking of Social Analysis.* Boston: Beacon Press.

Rosemary, P. (1991). "In Short: Postmodern Education." *Change* 23 (4): 55.

Rosen, S. (1975). "Measuring the Obsolescence of Knowledge." In F. T. Juster, *Education, Income, and Human Behavior.* New York: McGraw-Hill.

Rosenblum, S. (1985). *Involving Adults in the Educational Process.* San Francisco: Jossey-Bass.

Rudolph, F. (1962). *The History of the Undergraduate Curriculum.* San Francisco: Jossey-Bass.

Salvato, A. (1995). "UC Retreat Will Reinforce Need for Class Instruction." *The Cincinnati Enquirer* (October 31): 7A.

Sandeen, A. (1991). *The Chief Student Affairs Officer: Leader, Manager, Mediator, Educator.* San Francisco: Jossey-Bass.

Schaffer, S. (1992). "Reformation Comes to the University." *Journal of Higher Education Management* 8 (1): 7–12.

Schon, D. (1971). *Beyond the Stable State.* San Francisco: Jossey-Bass.

Senge, P. (1990). *The Fifth Discipline: The Art and Practice of the Learning Organization.* New York: Doubleday.

Shriberg, A. (1980). *Providing Student Services for the Adult Learner.* San Francisco: Jossey-Bass.

Simmons, D. (1995). "Retraining Dislocated Workers in the Community College: Identifying Factors for Persistence." *Community College Journal* 23 (2): 47–58.

Simons, J., and D. Fischer. (1995). "High Tech Karma." *U.S. News and World Report* 119 (8 August 21): 45–47.

Slaughter, S. (1991). "The 'Official' Ideology of Higher Education: Ironies and Inconsistencies." In W. Tierney, ed., *Culture and Ideology in Higher Education*, 59–86. New York: Praeger.

Smith, P. (1990). *Killing the Spirit.* New York: Viking Press.

Smith, T. (1993). *Dialectical Social Theory and Its Critics.* Albany: State University of New York Press.

Spretnak, C. (1988). "Postmodern Directions." In D. Griffin, ed., *Spirituality and Society: Postmodern Visions*, 33–40. Albany: State University of New York Press.

Spring, J. (1988). *Conflicts of Interest: The Politics of American Education.* New York: Longman.

Stephens, M. (1993). *Closing the Doors: Stories of Struggle at U.C.* A report prepared by the College of Arts and Sciences, University of Cincinnati.

Stoll, M. (1994). "What Is Multicultural Education?" *Community College Journal* 65 (3): 11–15.

Tierney, W. G. (1988). *The Web of Leadership.* Greenwich, Conn.: JAI Press.

———. (1989). *Curricular Landscapes, Democratic Vistas: Transformative Leadership in Higher Education.* New York: Praeger.

———, ed. (1991). *Culture and Ideology in Education.* New York: Praeger.

———. (1992). "Building Academic Communities of Difference." *Change* 42 (2): 40–46.

———. (1993). *Building Communities of Difference.* Westport, Conn.: Bergin & Garvey.

Tisdell, E. (1993a). "Feminism and Adult Learning." In S. Merriam, *An Update on Adult Learning Theory*, 91–104. New Directions for Adult and Continuing Education 57 (Spring). San Francisco: Jossey-Bass.

———. (1993b). "Interlocking Systems of Power, Privilege, and Class Oppression in Adult Education Classes." *Adult Education Quarterly* 43 (4): 203–226.

Uehling, B. (1992). "So Money is a Problem." *Journal of Higher Education Management* 7 (2): 7–14.

Usher, R. (1994). *Postmodernism and Education.* London: Routledge.

U.S. Department of Commerce. (1990). *Number of Inhabitants, Part 1, United States Summary.* Bureau of the Census. Series PC080–1, A1:1–35. Washington, D.C.: U.S. Government Printing Office.

Vernon, S., L. Lo Parco, and V. Marsick. (1993). "Satisfying Accountability Needs with Traditional Methods." In T. Heaney ed., *The Administration of Adult Education Programs*, 87–101. New Directions for Adult and Continuing Education 60 (Winter). San Francisco: Jossey-Bass.

Veysey, L. (1965). *The Emergence of the American University.* Chicago: University of Chicago Press.

Welton, M. (1993). "The Contribution of Critical Theory." In S. Merriam, *An Update on Adult Learning Theory*, 81–90. New Directions for Adult and Continuing Education 57 (Spring). San Francisco: Jossey-Bass.

Wheatley, M. (1992). *Leadership and the New Science.* San Francisco: Berrett-Koehler Publishers.

Wildavsky, A. (1971). *The Revolt against the Masses and Other Essays on Politics and Public Policy.* New York: Basic Books.

———. (1979). *The Politics of the Budgetary Process.* Boston: Little, Brown.

———. (1991). *The Rise of Radical Egalitarianism.* Washington, D.C.: American University Press.

Willets, J., M. Boyce, and C. A. Franklin. (1995). "Praxis as a New Method in the Academy." *Adult Learning* 6 (6): 10–11.

Williams, R. (1992). "Social Advocates and Action Learning: The Discontent Dancing with Hope," 37–49. In *New Directions for Adult and Continuing Education* 53 (Spring). San Francisco: Jossey-Bass.

Wilson, R. (1981). "The Courage to Be Leisured." *Social Forces* 60 (2): 282–303.

Wingard, E. (1995). "Student Services and the Adult Learner." *Network* (Cincinnati. The Union Institute) 12 (2): 35.

Wlodkowski, R. (1985). *Enhancing Adult Motivation to Learn: A Guide to Improving Instruction and Increasing Learner Achievement.* San Francisco: Jossey-Bass.

Wolin, R. (1992). *The Terms of Cultural Criticism: The Frankfurt School.* New York: Columbia University Press.

Wong, F. (1991). "Diversity and Community." *Change* 32 (4): 48–54.

Wright, R. (1995). "The Evolution of Despair." *Time* (August 28) 146 (9): 50–57.

Yearley, L. (1993). "Conflicts among Ideals of Human Flourishing." In G. Outka and J. Reeder, eds. *Prospects for a Common Morality*, 233–253. Princeton, N.J.: Princeton University Press.

Zaretsky, E. (1986). "Rethinking the Welfare State." In J. Dickinson and R. Russell, eds., *Family, Economy and State under Capitalism.* New York: St. Martin's Press.

Index

About the Author

TIMOTHY WILLIAM QUINNAN is Assistant Dean and Chief Student Affairs Officer at Raymond Walters College at the University of Cincinnati.

ISBN 0-89789-521-5

HARDCOVER BAR CODE